Indian Medical Science Series No. 161

SKIN CARE AND CURE IN AYURVEDA

Prof. Dr. P.H. Kulkarni

Sri Satguru Publications
A Division of
Indian Books Centre
Delhi, India

Published by

Sri Satguru Publications
A Division of
Indian Books Centre
24/4, Shakti Nagar, Near Dena Bank,
Delhi-110007

Email: ibcindia@vsnl.com
Website: http://www.indianbookscentre.com

First Edition; Delhi, 2007

ISBN 81-7030-852-6

Printed at Chawla Offset Printers, Delhi 110 052

CONTENTS

CHAPTER 1

HOLISTIC SKIN - CARE AND CURE ACCORDING TO AYURVEDA

Juliette Parkin
Adelaide, South Australia

Skin has many vital functions. This sense organ, or tactile organ starts functioning as birth takes place and is the largest eliminative organ, freeing the system of poisons. Many thousands of tiny sweat glands also act as a regulator of body temperature. Skin protected and insulates us from outside influences, like germs and insects etc., and protects the underlying organs. Skin is a major producer of endocrine hormones and contains thousands of cutaneous nerves that are connected to every part of the body. The skin is capable of understanding many types of touch qualities, like pleasurable sensation or pain, clod, heat, roughness, dryness, smoothness, hardness and softness. Softness of gulma (phantom tumour) and asmari (stone in the urinary tract) are examined by the physician by touch. Seasonal changes effect the colour and texture of skin, for instance, in the cool season skin is generally better and in the hot season skin becomes worse, with ulceration and skin cancer is some individuals in western countries. In this case, pastes of nimba, musta, manjishta, and chandan can be applied. In very hot countries, boils, pimples and itching with sweating is more common, and pastes of chandan, nimba, musta, manjistha and daruharidra are useful. Ayurveda describes seven layers of skin. The first layer is called avabhasini. It carries lasika (lymph) and vari (water). Diseases like padma kantaka (skin disease like thorns of a lotus stalk) and sidhma, are in this layer. It is 1/18th of a brihi. The second layer of the skin is called lohita dhara. Diseases like tila kalaka are located in this layer. It is 1/16th of a brihi. The third layer of skin is called sweda. The disease charma dala, itching eruptions is located in this layer. The fourth layer is called tamra. Diseases like kilasa and svitra (leucoderma) are located in this layer. The fifth layer is called vedini. Diseases like kustha (obstinate skin diseases like leprosy). Dadru (ring worm) and gajacarna are located in this layer. It is 1/5th of a brihi. The sixth layer is called lohita. Diseases like galaganda (tumour on side of neck or goitre), gandamala (swelling of the glands of the neck), balmika and slipada (elephantiasis) etc., are located in this layer. In size it is like a brihi. The seventh layer, which is very thick, is called mamsa dhara. Diseases like vidradhi (abscess), bhagandara (fistula–in ano) and arsas (piles) are located in this layer. In size it is like two brihis taken together. The thickness of the skin is equal to the thickness of two barley grains, and the thickness of angustha (thumb). Skin undergoes a continuous process of regeneration and simultaneously the superficial layer are peeled off. Therefore, the body requires a constant supply of nutrition.

The Ayurvedic approach to healthy skin involves balance and harmony on the spiritual, mental and physical levels. A balanced diet and a positive mental attitude will show a healthy skin. Sadhana practices and yoga (pranayama and asanas) will calm the mind and envigorate the body, helping it to eliminate waste products efficiently, giving a healthy glow to the skin. Ideal skin is oily, smooth, soft, thin, shiny and lustrous white deep rooted hairs. When there is skin disease there will be discoloration or abnormal variations.

The skin is a true mirror of the internal state of an individual, reflecting the condition of the heart, brain, stomach, blood, spleen, as well as the emotions. The appearance and complexion of the skin are influenced by the nervous system, and many emotions such as anger, fear, guilt, excitement, grief, shock etc., will show a red, mottled, blackish, flushed, pale pasty colour on the skin.

There is no disease in which aggravated doshas do not play their role. In diseases of Kapha there is itching over the body. Vayu will show bluish stains along with roughness and black colouration of nails, and with Pitta there is sweating, yellow colouration of face, nails, eyes, skin, urine and stools.

Many disturbances of body, mind and soul are recorded on the skin surface, so it is important that a person explores ways in which to balance the mind, through meditation, relaxation, music etc. to maintain equilibrium. The condition of Agni, or digestive fire, is of vital importance in Ayurveda, should the Agni be impaired in some way, the skin will show imbalances like discolouration, dryness, redness or rashes, boils, pimples, herpes, oozing, swelling, hyperpigmentation and kustha etc. A balanced diet of fresh vegetables and fruit, especially amalaka, dried black grapes, figs, dates and pomegranate; ghee, honey, rice etc. and the use of spices like ginger, black pepper, pippali, turmeric, cummin, ajwan, coriander, black mustard seed and garlic, will aid digestion and keep the body fresh. Excessive intake of hot things, sour and salty foods, spicy things, tea, coffee alcohol and tobacco will cause toxins production, spots and blackness on the skin. Drug addiction and smoking will cause a change in the colour of skin also.

Taking food at the correct time each day, eating food suited to the needs of your prakriti or constitution, adjusting the diet to seasonal changes, and not taking more food than the body needs, will keep the digestive fire in order. When Agni is performing properly, the rakta dhatu is then formed correctly and there will not be formation of impure blood. Rakta dhatu and Raktavaha srotas and their correct function, is very important for skin, being balancing for skin and keeping good blood. Good circulation of blood is important to the skin and whole body. Vyana Vayu Mahabhuta is related to skin, with Bhrajaka pitta responsible for lustre of the skin, and the responsible agent for the conversion, at the skin level, of therapeutic oil and maintenance of the complexion. Due to Dhatusar, the skin is of good natural colour.

The Role of Oja in the Maintenance of Healthy Skin

Oja plays a vital role in the health of a person and a healthy complexion depends on the correct formation of oja. When health problems are studied we must automatically look at oja which encompasses the physical, mental and spiritual aspects of a human being. Oja is the excellent essence of the seven dhatus, or bodily tissues. The first and foremost formation in human life is that of oja, formed in the foetus and later on is formed from the finest part of the seven dhatus, Rasa, Rakta, Mamsa, Meda, Ashthi, majja, shukra and strength (mental) of the body. Life span, complexion and general health are largely determined by the nutrient semen or ovum. Oja is localized in the heart and its potency and power are diffused to all parts of the body. It is responsible for all the activities going on in the body. Even though the three doshas, Vata, Pitta and Kapha are in equilibrium in the body, they are unable to function without oja. Oja is the ultimate result of food that has reached through to Shukra dhatus, but the first dhatu, Rasa, must have some 'force' for this cycle to end successfully. When the seven dhatus, from Rasa to Shukra, go through a healthy development, with each and every dhatu nourished, the result will be ooja. Destruction of oja leads to destruction of the body. When there is correct formation of oja, the complexion is fair and immunity strong, with firmness, freshness, steadiness and growth in the dhatus.

Tranquility of mind is the main element which increases oja, therefore one should engage in something which is liked by the individual and gives pleasure to the mind. Food excelling in characteristics which increase oja are : Madhur (sweet), Snigdha (moist), Sheet (cold), Laghu (that which is light on the stomach).

Food and plants which are said to be ojavardhak are : milk, butter, cream of milk, ghrita (ghee), black gram, white pumpkin, grapes, dates, Liquorice Root (glycyrrhiza glabra), Ashwagandha (withania sonmifera), Shatavari (asparagus racemosus) and Guduchi (tinorspora cordifolia) etc.

In rare individuals, oja, which is not normally visible, will be seen like a light or sunshine on the face, eyes and around the head of a person. This unusual quality in the complexion is the result of oja and will depend on the right food and moral behaviour of a person. Only when there is sound health and mind will oja show. It is there when a person takes sattvic food and does not succumb, at any time, to the six enemies of the mind *i.e.,* ego, anger, jealousy, temptation, lust and greed. Therefore, a highly moral person will show oja. When exceptionally gifted people transform oja into spiritual strength, having achieved self-realization, this peculiar, luminous light, a shadowless light, or divine light, can be seen on the complexion. We have only to look at the faces of saints like Swami Vivekananda, Parmahansa

Yogananda, Ramdas, Tulsidas etc., to see this halo, or light, captivating in its message of purity and blissfulness. In contrast, a person who has not reached this stage of perfection will show a black colour on the face with different emotions. For example, a person who has experienced mental shock, or who has a small amount of guilt will not have the shine of oja on their face.

Although this exalted state and consequent unusual complexion is exceptional, keeping oja balanced and promoting its nourishment in the body is essential for a healthy body, mind and complexion.

Preventative Care of Skin–External Treatment

Dry Massage (Udvartana) Body Cleansing

The body breathes through the skin, absorbing oxygen and exhaling carbon dioxide. Fresh air and keeping the body clean is important. Occasional use of a soft, dry, bristle brush and lightly brushing the body to remove some of the millions of dead blood cells, which become clogged on the skin surface, is useful. This will avoid uric acid and other impurities, that are normally excreted through the skin, not to remain in the body where the kidneys will be overworked and the system poisoned. Cleansing the skin with dry powders stimulates circulation, is useful for liquification of fat, removal of Kapha and bad odour. It makes children's skin soft and gives firmness and strength to the underlying tissues. Some powders that are beneficial for the skin are :

- Chick pea flour
- Kapur Kachari Powder
- Musta Powder
- Turmeric Powder

– Amalaki Powder

– Chandan Powder

LEPA (Paste application) with Varnya qualities (giving good complexion).

– Chick pea flour.
– Amalaki powder
– Camphor + chandan + turmeric
– Khus powder
– Chandan mixed with rose water
– Chandan
– Manjishta powder
– Neem Powder

Abhyanga (Oil Massage)

Skin can absorb nutrients, vitamins, minerals, and oils and proteins can be assimilated into the system when applied directly to the skin, with Vitamin D produced directly on the skin by the action of sunrays and then absorbed into the body.

Oil massage makes the skin feel warm and supple and alleviates Vayu. It soothes the nervous system and endocrine system and rejuvenates the skin. Regular oil massage to the body increases resistance to infection and bacteria through the skin, increases muscle tone and stability to the body, relieves fatigue, cleans and strengthens skin, promotes health, eliminates, impurities, provides nutrition to the hair follicles, benefits sleep when applied to the head and benefits the eyes when put on the soles of the feet. The heat that massage produces helps skin below the surface, keeps old age at bay, helps weakness, over–exertion and improves general well-being. Oil massage can cure some diseases of the skin and produces sturdiness of the legs. There is an increase in tissue elements with regular massage.

Samvahana or Mardana

Samvahana, or the pressing or kneading of the body with the hands or feet, often undertaken after an oil massage, is comforting and soothing and especially helpful to weak people who are first massaged with Bala oil, followed by kneading. This helps to tone muscles, assisting the stability of the body, and improves complexion and sleep. Pressing also help to mobilise waste products and prevents local accumulation of excessive Kapha.

Dry skin needs snehana, along with swedana and Bruhana (internal treatment) to balance Vayu. Oils that are frequently used in Ayurveda are :

- Sesame Oil.
- Almond Oil.
- Coconut Oil.
- Mustard Oil.
- Ground Nut Oil.
- Narayan Oil.

These oils can be medicated (Siddha) according to the different diseases. Oils are sedative in nature and are used in conditions of pain, or purfumed for relaxation.

After an oil massage, it is useful to wait half–an–hour before taking a hot bath. Before bathing, one of the following powders or pastes can be used to rub on the body : Chandan, Amalaki, Turmeric, Vekhanda, Khus, Chick pea, Nagarmotha or Manjishtha.

Abhyanga is not given if Jatharagni is not working correctly, otherwise the pores will not be open; during fevers (ama cause), vitiation of Kapha, after the 5 purificatory procedures, or when there is indigestion.

It is important to start massage at an early age so the pleasurable and healing powers of abhyanga can be experienced and a good habit formed early in life.

Shirodhara treatment, in which warm sesame oil is dripped in a stream on to the forehead to relax the nervous system and balance prana vayu, is especially useful in cases of insomnia or nervous tension.

Baths–Hot/Cold/Sauna

Baths give energy and strength and are calming and soothing to the body and mind. Baths are healthy for skin as they relax a tired, over–worked body and are beneficial after exercise. The steam and heat in hot baths causes sweating which opens the pores and rids the body of impurities and bad odours. Itching, caused by dirt on the skin, it relieved by a bath. Heaviness, exhaustion and sleepiness are reduced and one feels energized and fresh after a bath. Cold water can bring up gastric fire. Warm baths have a vata Shamak effect, are relaxing and reduce thirst. Warm or cold baths can be used depending on the climate. A healthy person can take a warm or hot bath, but not hot or chilled water should not be used on the head. Baths should be avoided when there is fever, asthma diarrhoea, bad digestive disorders, flatulence and after food has been taken. After taking a bath one should properly clean the body with a piece of cloth.

Conclusion

Preventative care is an important factor in Ayurvedic

skin care. A healthy diet and life–style, and proper mind coordination will help a person avoid skin problems and many diseased states.

The skin is a sensitive organ and is continuously exposed to various environmental stresses such as, varying temperatures, dust, smoke, heat, cold, rain and wind etc. so it is important to take good care of the skin and maintain its healthy condition.

BIBLIOGRAPHY

DASH, Bhagwan and KASHYAP, *Basic Principles of Ayurveda*, Naurang Rai, Concept Publishing Co. New Delhi 110015, India.

CHARAKA/SUSHRUTA/VAGBHATA (Astang Hrdaya).

CHAPTER 2

CLINICAL EVALUATION OF AYURVEDIC DRUGS ON VITILIGO (LEUCODERMA)

Dr. C.R. Karnick
Research Scientist
Clinical and Experimental Division,
Ayurvedic Research, Wockhardt Limited,
Aurangabad.

Abstract

India is rich in herbal flora and fauna and abounds in about 2000 species, from high altitude of Himalayas (temperate) to vast areas of tropical forests in South East, with flat lands traversed by mighty rivers of Brahmaputra, Ganga, Indus, Godavari, Tapi, Krishna and Cavery, rich in herb and medical flora with various varieties and types spreading in various climatic zones.

Most of the herbs are being used by physicians of Indian system of Medicine, (Ayurveda, Unani, Siddha).

Of the common in decoloration affecting 3% of population by vitiligo. This paper records for the first time the effect of herbal drugs on Vitiligo. The results are promising nearly 60 to 65% show positive results and cure of white spots in a span ranging from 3 months to an year.

Introduction

Vitiligo or Leucoderma is an enigmatic disorder. It is common in coastal areas of Indian Subcontinent and parts of the world. The incidence is about 3 to 4% of the Indian population in comparison with about one percent for the world population.

Vitiligo (leucoderma) is declined as a circumscribed, acquired idiopathic, progressive hypomelanoses of skin and hair, often familiar and characterised by a total absence of melanocytes microscopically. The defination excludes post–inflammatory chemically induced depigmentation and depigmentation associated with melanoma, and secondary to various other dermatoses.

Its aetiology remains obscure and successful treatment has always been a challenge to the medical world.

Formation of Melanin in the Skin

The biology of melanin formation has been widely studied and summerised by Fitzpatrick *et. al.,* (1967).

Skin colour is related to the number and distribution of the subcellular units of melanin formation namely the structured specialized brown organells, melanosomes, that are formed in and secreted by melanocytes.

Melano becomes bear a copper containing enzyme, tyrosina, which catalyzes the oxidation of tyrosine to indole–5,–6 quinone. This quinone along with other tyrosine intermediate, polymerizes into highly insoluble substance that is strongly bound to proteins through sulfhydril–linkage. Melanin polymers absorb the ultraviolet and visible spectra. Melanoprotein is extremely dense.

Melanin pigmentation takes place in the epidermal melanin unit which is defined as a melanocyte surrounded by a constellation of malpighian cells.

The number of melanosomes produced and the rates of their transfer to malpighan cells are regulated partly by hormones and ultraviolet light, but primarily by genetic factors, malpighan cells themselves may provide clues for melanocytic activity.

Efficacy and Safety of Ayurvedic Cream and Capsule in the Treatment of Vitiligo

Table 1 : Baseline Profile of Patients

No. of patients	
– Enrolled	63
– Dropouts	22
– Completed (partially/fully)	41
Sex	
Males	21
Females	20
Age (years)	
Mean	29.3
S.E.M.	2.13
History of Vitiligo	
Maternal	5
Paternal	8
None	20

* S.E.M. = Standards Error of Means.

Table 2 : Distribution of Patients by Occupation

	No. of Patients (%)
Household Work	13
Students	10
Telephone Operators	8

[*Contd...*]

Farm Workers	5
Others @	5
Total	41

@ Others include workers from Chemical Factory, Rubber mfg units etc.

Table 3 : Efficacy by Duration of Treatment

Treatment Duration (months)	*No. of pts.*	*Investigator's Opinion*				*% Responders*
		Responders			*Non-Responders*	
		Exc.	*Good*	*Poor*	*Poor*	
1	5	0	0	2	3	20%
2	4	0	0	2	2	50%
3	4	0	0	2	2	50%
4	4	0	1	2	1	75%
5	4	0	2	1	1	75%
6/More	20	1	9	8	2	90%
Total	41	1	12	17	11	73%

Success Rate with 6 months complete treatment .... 90%.
Overall success rate with duration of treatment between 1 and 6 months 73%

Table 4 : Efficacy Pts Defaulting before 6 months of Treatment

Treatment Duration (months)	*No. of pts.*	*Investigator's Opinion*			*Without Response*	*% Responders*
		Exc.	*Good*	*Poor*		
1	5	0	0	2	3	20%
2	4	0	0	2	2	50%
3	4	0	0	2	2	50%
4	4	0	21	2	1	75%
5	4	0	2	1	1	75%
Total (1-5 months)	21	0	3	9	9	57%

[*Contd...*]

6 or more	20	1	9	8	2	90%
Total (1-6 months)	40	1	12	17	11	73%

Success Rate with 6 months complete treatment 90%

Overall success rate with duration of treatment between 1 and 6 months 73%

Table 5 : Efficacy–Pts completing 6 months Treatment

Response	*No. of Pts. (%)*
Excellent	1 (5)
Good	9 (45)
Fair	8 (40)
Poor	2 (10)
Total	20 (100)

Table 6 : Response : Sitewise

Part of Body	*No. of Total*	*Lesions*	*% Improved*
Face and Head	22	15	68
Neck	11	5	45
Upper Limb	32	15	47
Lower Limb	38	17	45
Chest and Abdomen	20	8	40
Back	17	11	65
Total	140	71	51%

Table 7 : Side Effects

Signs and Symptoms	*No. of Pts.*
Redness of patch	3
Burning of eyes	1
Bulbers eruption	1

CHAPTER 3

SAFE REMEDIAL MEASURE FOR TREATMENT OF INFLAMMATION OF MUCOUS MEMBRANCE OF MOUTH TONGUE AND LIPS

Dr. N.D. Panchabhai
C/97, Kotyarknagar-4,
Behind Ajwa Road Water tank,
Opp. Muncipal School, Baroda-390019

Physiology and Anatomical Aspect

Anatomically oral mucous membrane, tongue and lips are having superficial layers of stratified squamous epithelium cells of compact type. The basic layers contain more connective tissues, especially the lips have strong basic connective tissues, these cells are very compact and flexible in action. The pigment tissues are more concentrated in the oral mucous membrane. (The chromatophores (pigment cells) are dense in the lips.

The oral mucous membrane of lips and tongue have special functions for various activities. In the digestive system the intake of food and supporting the food material for chewing and diverting the same to oesophagus, also sensory functions are performed by tongue (m. m. of the tongue) part of the alkaline digestion and absorption takes place in the mouth cavity.

Due to various etiological factors, the oral mucous membrane is inflamed. The inflammation of the oral mucous membrane is termed as "stomatitis".

Stomatitis occurs mainly due to the deficiency of vitamin B complex and liver insufficiency as per the Allopathic opinion. As per the ancient Ayurvedic literature 65 types of Mukh–Rogas occur due to various reasons. Main reason is "KAPHADOSHAM" Some of the other reasons are described as under.

(*a*) Hot and tingling taste food hot drinks etc. affect the temperature, ph etc. in the mouth cavity, repeated consumption of such foods or habits causes inflammation of the oral mucous membrane and tongue. Also drying of the lips, burning etc. develops.

(*b*) Due to KAPHA–DOSHA and liver insufficiency.

(*c*) Eating too much of tobacco for long duration or heavy smoking for many years, leads to inflammation of the oral mucous membrane. In chronic cases ulceration and hardening of tissues (Fibrosis) can be seen.

(*d*) Vitamin deficiency due to non–eating green leafy vegetables and fruits (NATURAL RAW FOOD) *e.g.*, cabbage, tomato, cucumber, green coriander, raw turmeric, carrot etc.

(*e*) Carelessness in cleaning teeth, mouth cavity, habit of bed tea etc. may cause infective type of stomatitis.

Etiological factors described above are not sufficient, even harmonal deficiencies and adrenal insufficiency may cause stomatitis and other problems, further studies are required to find out the etiological problems.

Lesions

1. Due to inflammation of the oral mucous membrane, in the initial stages, congestion is seen in the affected area.

   As the condition aggressive, exposure of inner soft tissues due to casting off of epithelial cells can be seen, also slight swelling and pain is associated the primary stage. The inflammed part of mucous membrane when comes in contact with food material, hot or cold drinks causes irritation.

2. Ulceration is predominant in chronic cases. Generally the ulceration results due to delay in treatment.

3. *White patches or fibrosis* : In case of tobacco eaters, the particular part where the tobacco is kept with lime or without lime, in the mouth to tobacco chewing, fibrous tissues develop in the area. Same may happen with a chain–smoker. Constant stimulation of particular part in the mouth cavity leads to fibrosis.

4. Suppuration is possible in infective type of stomatitis; a very rare condition.

5. Cracks on the lips can be seen in stomatis, also due to the change of the climate.

Treatment

Many treatments have been prescribed in various pathies depending upon symptoms and intensity of stomatitis. We have tried to develop a safe non–toxic medicine "Stomacel". Stomacel has given 100% result in ordinary, occasional stomatitis in children and adults. It is also useful in treatment of mouth ulcers and fibrosis of mouth mucous membrane to certain extent.

The details of the ingredient of "Stomacel" are as under–

1. **Anacyclus Perethrum** : In ancient Ayurvedic literatures, the properties of Aakkalak have been described as "Kapha–Nashak"–It also cures mouth diseases, these properties are attributed due to the pellitorine or pyretin containsts of the herb. Chemical structure of which is C 4 H25 N O (N–isobutile deca–trans–2–trans–4–diaenamide).

2. **Camphore** : C 10 H 16 O–Available from cinnamomom camphora tree : found most suitable in the treatment of stomatitis, in very low concentration–It acts as a counter irritant, mild antiseptic. Studies reveal that M.L.D. in rats is 2.2 gm. per kg. The concentration of 0.01% is non–toxic and also effective in the treatment of stomatitis.

3. **Papaver Somniferum** : The seeds content fixed oils and albuminoids. Albuminoids are proteins. The extract has soothing effect on the mucous membrane.

4. **Myristica Frangans** : Main containt is trimyristin, has mild stimulent and aromatic properties.

5. **Glycyrrhiza Glabra** : The main content is Glycyrrhizin, 6 to 14%. It is demulscent. It helps in curing the mouth ulcers and also removes the Kapha–Dosha.

6. **Acecia Catechu** : Derived from the heart wood of acecia catechu. Chemical analysis reveals that it contains 25 to 30% catechu–tannic acid, 2 to 10% catechin. It is astringent in action, healing, mild stimulent and helps in mild contraction of oral mucous membrane, especially in mouth ulcers much useful.

7. **Jasmine Leaves :** A ketone is found in the Jasmine Leaves, Jasmone, C11 H16 O, organic combination is 3–methyl–2–2–pentenyl–2–cyclopenten–1. As per the ayurvedic literatures ext. of Uthica patram helps in curing the mouth mucous membrane inflammation. Helps in healing m. m. ulcers. It gives firmness to mouth mucous membrane.
8. **Oleum Sesamum Indicum :** (Sesame Oil)–It contains olein, stearin, palmitin, linolein, myristin, Sesamin, sesamolin esters of fatty acids. It is a Best vehicle/medium for medicine. It softens the oral mucous membrane mildly. It also softens the lip–tissues in case of dry lips or lip crack conditions.
9. **Cinnamomam Zeylanicum :** The ext. contains 80 to 90% Cinnamaldehide and cinnamyl acetate. it acts as a mild stimulent, also cures Kapha condition, useful in treatment of all mukhrogam as per the opinion of Ayurbhishak.
10. **Berberis Aristata :** The dried stem of the Indian berbery. Main chemical ingredient is Berberine, C22 G19 NO5 5.5 H2O. it is febrifuse, carminative, also useful in dressing of the mouth ulcers in low concentration. It acts as an excellent safe antiseptic.
11. **Azadirachta Indica (Margosa) :** Contains mostly glycerides and nimbdin, nimbin, nimbidiol alkaloids. Acts as an excellent antiseptic in the treatment of m.m. ulcers.
12. **Philanthus Embleca, Myrobellan Bleric, Terminalia Chhebula :** The ext exerts the properties of antiseptic, soothing effect on the oral mucous membrane.

13. **Alumen** : Binds the ext. in the medium, also acts as an antiseptic and helps in the healing process of mouth lesions.

All these ingredients are extracted in the base of oil of sesame and preserved. The process of extracting is done at low temperature and standed for 24 hrs. thereafter the containts are filtered and packed in the bottles, in hygienic condition.

Method of Use

Stomcel is to be applied to the lesions of oral mucous membrane with cleaned fingers and the patient was asked to spread the medicine with help of movement of tongue in the mouth cavity, after 15 to 20 minutes gargling with luke warm water was advised.

Recommended Application of Stomacel in Various M.M. Problems

1. 5 drops to be applied twice daily for 2 to 5 days in ordinary, occasional stomatitis.
2. 5 drops 4 times daily in ulcerative stomatitis, for 30 days.
3. 5 drops 5 to 6 times daily in fibrosis cases for long duration, average 2 to 3 months.

The stomacel after application should be moved/spreaded in the mouth cavity with movement of the tongue; after 15 to 20 minutes, gurgling with luke–warm water is advised for spitting out the applied medication. Even if stomacel is swallowed through oversight by children or adult no side effect is observed. The medication has been tested for toxicity and found that it is non–toxic.

Trials

60 cases of different age groups, having problems of inflammation of oral mucous membrane were supplied stomacel with necessary instructions as advised above depending upon type of symptoms.

The Results were as under

1. *Age group 8 to 12 years (12 cases) :* All having symptom of ordinary stomatitis. Advise was given as per the recommended dose described above.

   Complete cure was resulted in 3 to 5 days.

2. Age group 13 years and above up to 30 years of age–(20 cases).

   Stomatitis and also inflammation of tongue was observed in 9 cases.

   Complete cure was observed in 5 to 7 days.

3. Age group 31 to 45 years–(20 cases).

   Tobacco chewers having mouth ulceration were specifically selected. Advise was given as per the recommended dose described earlier.

   11 cases were cured, who reduced tobacco consumption during the coarse to treatment. Result was not encouraging in cases were tobacco chewing was continued during the coarse of treatment.

   During of treatment was for 30 to 60 days.

   Inference : Tobacco chewing be reduced during the coarse of treatment.

4. Age group 45 years and above — (8 cases).

   Stomititis was cured in 3 cases where no habit of tobacco chewing or smoking.

Ulceration/fibrosis case shown improvement in opening of mouth in 2 months, (3 cases).

Very little or negligible improvement observed in 2 cases, may be termed as no improvement.

General Observation

Repeatation of the treatment was not required in cured cases. Orally, Triphala churna was advised in cases where constipation was one of the symptom associated with stomatitis.

Conclusion

1. Normal/occasional stomatitis is cured in 3 to 5 days.
2. Deficiency type stomatitis/difficulty in swallowing of food was corrected in most of the cases, when gurgling with luke–warm water mixed with 10 drops of stomacel was done, this aspect still needs detailed studies.
3. Ulcer/patches/fibrosis need long duration of treatment.
4. Very little or no improvement was seen in cases where the tobacco eating was continued during the treatment.

   No specific instruction was given for diet/food during a course of treatment.
5. Lip cracks/winter lip cracks were cured by application of stomacel in 5 cases, however the trial is not sufficient, further trial is going on.

"STOMACEL" is an attempt towards treatment of stomatitis, a common problem, by safe non–toxic method. More work is still required to be done in this aspect, especially for treatment of chronic ulcers and fibrosis.

CHAPTER 4

EFFICACY OF "ROMASANJANANA LEPA" ['KARANJA', 'KASISA', 'KAPITTHA'] IN REGENERATION OF HAIR IN 'INDRALUPTA' (ALOPECIA)

Dr. Deodatta Sitaram Bhadlikar
Lecturer in Y.M.T. Ayurved Medical College,
Currey Rd., Mumbai-12.
Dr. K.S. Kulkarni & Dr. G.S. Lavekar

The Indian Medicine "Ayurveda" is omni–potent a treasure of all aspects of Health and disease. In present scientific era many aspects of "Ayurveda" are coming in view under the light of scientific developments. In the "Ayurvedic" texts all surgical aspect are described such as preventive, promotive, curative. Apart from this the cosmetic aspect is most important particularly in post surgical conditions.

The aim of this cosmetological branch of surgery is to eliminate, minimise or normalise the post surgical scar, discolouration, loss of hair etc. These measures are equally effective in post surgical or similar disease condition. "Sushruta" known as the father of Indian surgery who is the first plastic surgeon. In the "Shasti–Upakrama" of "Sushruta" he has intentionally avoided surgery and advised 'Upakrama' like application of paste in the treatment of 'Indralupta' (Alopecia).

Keeping the same view in mind the great' Sushruta' in his treatment of "Indralupta" (Alopecia) avoided major surgery *i.e.,* Hair Transplantation which is so painful, most of the time not very successful and with post surgical complications. The hair on an individual's scalp and body is his personal mark. Taking care of the normal scalp and the hair is the day to day attention given by us to maintain its health and to increase its beauty. Now a day people are using so many cosmetics, lotions, creams, soaps, shampoos in order to make their hair look more beautiful. In both male and female there is a tendency to hide their age. Loss of hair gives an appearance of more age than the actual age of the individual.

Hair contributes one's personality and has always remained the centre of attraction. So each one is extra conscious about it and is in search of better remedy for their growth and glory. Since the drawbacks of modern medicines are evident, there is utmost need of cheap, non-toxic, non-irritant, easily available herbals 'Ayurvedic' product. Preparations are described for Ramasanjanana (Hair regeneration) but this 'Karanja', 'Kasisa', 'Kapittha' lepa is simple, cost effective, preparation exclusively advocate locally on scalp. On sound scientific basis, the attempt is made to establish the efficacy of hair regeneration.

About Clinical Study of Drug

Large number of drugs for the regeneration of hair both herbal and mineral components as well as single drugs have been described in ancient "Ayurvedic" texts.

The purpose of this study is to re–establish the use of 'Romasanjanana Lepa' in regeneration of scalp hair in particular.

"Romasanjanana Lepa"

'Lepa Kalpana' (mode of application of paste locally) made up of three constituents taken in equal quantity.

	Name of Ingredients	*Used Part*
1.	'Karanja' (pongmia glabra)	'patra' (leaf)
2.	'Kasisa' (ferrous sulphate^{FeSO47HO2O})	plain 'Kasisa'
3.	'Kapittha' (feronia elephuntum)	fruit.

"Kasisa" ($FeSO_4 7H_2O$) Ferrous Sulphate

Properties : Astringent or styphic, acidic, hot and reduces deranged 'Vata and Kapha', Haematinic and tonic without any odour soluble in water, but insoluble in alcohol.

Therapeutic Uses : In healing ulcers, skin disease, Improves skin complexion, cures leucoderma and other skin ailments, it produces normal pigmentation of hair dyes.

'Kapittha' (Feronia Elephantum Correa)

Family–Rutacae–'Bilvadivarga'

Species–Indo–Malayan

A monotypic genus of indo–malayan region represented by F.Limonia.

– F. Limonia (Linn.) Swingle syn.

– F. Elephantum correa.

A small deciduous tree–fruit large Lobose or oblate 1.0 to 2.5 inches in diameter with hard, rough, woody, pericarp seeds. Numerous small compressed embedded in sweetish aromatic edible pulp.

Types–Two

1. Small acidic fruits.
2. Large Sweet fruits.

Properties–Ripe fruit is sour, sweet in flavour and taste, astringent, aphrodiasiac reduces deranged 'Doshas' *i.e.,* 'Vata, Pitta'. After digestion it converts in katu–vipaka (pungent secretion/juice state) and having property of 'Shitavirya' (cooling in nature) cooling action is attributed to its 'Shitavirya'.

Therapeutic uses–Reduces blood impurities, aromatic, Antidote to poisons, appetiser, diuretic. Chemical Composition : Analysis of edible part (55–58%) of fruit gave following values.

Moisture	69.5
Protein	7.3
Ether. extr.	0.6
Mineral matter	1.9
Fibre	5.2
Carbohydratc	15.5
Calcium	0.13
Phosphorus	0.11%
Iron	0.6 mg/100 gm
Riboflavin	170 micrograms/ 100 gm
Vit. C	2.0 mg/100 gm

Wood apple is rich in mineral constituents of the pulp and varies from 7.6% in unripe fruits to 2.3% in fully ripe ones. It contains 3–5% pectin.

'Karanja' Patra (Pongamia glabra rent or Glednpa Indica)

Family–Papilionaceae

Species–Indo–Malayan

P. glabra rent is used medicinally in china, Indo–China, Philippine islands, Australia.

A medium sized glabrous tree, leaves, imperipinnate leaflets 5–7 ovate or elliptic. Six types of tree.

Properties : Bitter taste, pungent, hot ('Ushana'), sharp ('Tikshana'), light ('Laghu') reduces 'Kapha, Vata, Pitta' ailments, 'Karanja' 'Patra' after digestion it converts in 'Katu Vipaka' (pungent state), purgative, increases 'pitta'.

Therapeutic Uses : Useful in 'Raktaj Vikar' (Blood diseases) and 'Pittaj Vikar (Pittaj Diseases)' and also useful in infectious diseases. A poultice of the leaves is applied on ulcers. The decoction of the leaves is used in medicated baths and fomentation's in cases of Rheumatic pains. The leaves are much resorted to as a domestic remedy in the treatment in diseases in children. Leaves destroy vegetable and animal parasites in skin diseases. Leaves are also cholagogue. Leaves are also used in diarrhoea, cough, dyspepsia. In Leprosy leaves of 'Karanja' and 'Citraka' (Plumbago Zeylanica Linn.) mixed with pepper and salt are powdered and given with curd, leaves are applied on bleeding piles locally.

Chemical Composition : Leaves are lopped for fodder and are said to act as galactogogue. They are rich in nitrogen and contain 7.19 mg/100 gm of carotene.

They are popular as green manure for rich and sugarcane, area gardens and coffee plantation.

Manurial value of the leaves and twigs are respectively : nitrogen 1.16, 0.71 phosphorus (P_2O_5) 0.14, 0.11, potash (K_2O) 0.49, 0.62, and lime (CaO) 1.54, 1.58% green manuring with the leaves is reported to reduce the incidence of root–knot of tomato caused by meloidogyne javanica. Extracts of the leaves were against micrococcus pyogeres varalureus.

Materials and Methods

For the clinical study 20 patients were selected between age group 0 to 60 years of both sexes. Constituents of "Romasanjanana Lepa" were taken in equal quantity, (Presumed according to 'Sharangdhara') by the reference of 'Anukta Mana'.

Trial Procedure/Assessment of efficacy : The efficacy of trial preparation was assessed on the basis of following criteria.

1. Permanent ink outline of the affected area was traced on butter paper of standard A_4 size was taken on 0th day indicating zero % of the re–growth of hair. Thus total patch which was taken equivalent to 100%. The regeneration of hair was divided accordingly and improvement was graded graphically.
2. The length of regenerated hair was measured in millimeter scale (mm) 0th, 14th, 28th. and 42nd day or last day *i.e.,* 84 day of treatment for comparison.
3. Each patient was screened on 0th and 42nd day or last day *i.e.,* 84th day for comparison with their initial status.
4. Changes in following signs and symptoms were recorded.

Dryness, Roughness, cleanness, Itching, Secretions, Unctuousness, Swelling, Blackish, Yellowish, Hot, Cool, any other discolouration.

The overall assessment of therapeutic effect is made on 4 point scale in the conclusion. The 'Romasanjanana' drug was mixed with coconut oil or water and Lepa was applied on the affected part in the morning and evening (2 times per day). The lepa was kept on affected part till it dried. Dosage : One fourth 'Angul', ('Angul' *i.e.,* 'Ayurvedic' unit for measurement) thick. 'Lepa' was applied on affected part as advised by 'Sarangadhara'.

The 'Chakrapanidatta' has advocated of paste for minimum period of 7 days. In the treatment of 'Indralupta' (Alopecia) Using the same unit (7 days) was multiplied to it. The 'Lepa' was applied on the affected part and response was assessed.

Criteria for Rejection of Patient

Patient with common systemic diseases, Alopecia developed due to burns, acids, chemicals, caustics, wounds on scalp, neoplasm and Radiation hazards, Congenital ectodermal defects or disorders, drug induced hair loss, generalised hair loss, above Age of 60 years were avoided.

Clinical Examinations

1. The examination of "Indralupta" (alopecia) was done by inspection ('Darshana') palpation ('Sparshara') and interrogation ('Prashna method).
2. General examination of the patient and local examination of affected part was done according to 'Samprapti' (Aetiopathology of disease) of "Indralupta") (Alopecia).
3. The clinical examination included investigation with special reference to 'Asthivaha strotasa, and 'Asthidhatu Status'. ('Ayurvedic' method of investigation of system of bones).

Lab Examination

CBC, ESR, Urine (Routine and microscopy) examination were done to exclude systemic diseases.

Parameter for analysis of hair distribution on treated patches and calculation of the approximate area of patches on initial and final day were measured on the following criteria :

Area of circle = $3.14 \times (\text{Radius})^2$

Area of square = $(\text{Side})^2$

Area of Rectangle = Length × width.

Sample : I have taken 10×10 mm^2 of normal healthy person as sample for finding out normal frequency of hair distribution per 100 mm^2 area. After analysis, I came, to conclusion that there are approximately 200 hairs per 100 mm^2 means 50 hairs per 25 mm^2. Therefore for calculating hair distribution on treated patches I have considered 25 mm^2 area (5×5 mm^2) as a standard base.

The tolerance was assessed on baseline symptoms and signs and symptoms develop during their trial with their nature, duration and severity in the record to find out unwanted effect of preparation.

Statistical Analysis

The data after collection was tabulated and statistically analysed using appropriate tests to study the significance.

Observation and Results

The improvement in positive formation of hair on previously bald patches and improvement in symptomatology is expressed in terms of percentage of result in the total grades of the complete of area of patches on '0' day and final day to evaluate the effect of 'Romasanjanana Lepa' in disease 'Indralupta' (Alopecia)–In this clinical study the average frequency of hair distribution in 20 cases of patchy hair loss of scalp region and including one patch of chin (beard) in "Indralupta" (Alopecia) disease were 3332 hair/ 67 patches that means 49.73 hair per 25 mm^2 area.

The efficacy of drug = 49.73 × 100/50 = 99.46%. This drug was found also effective in patchy hair loss psoriasis. The maximum average rate of growth was found in 2nd inspection period *i.e.*, 15th day to 28th day which is 0.7 mm/ day. The average rate of growth of hair at the end of 42nd day was 0.59 mm/day.

Discussion

"Indralupta" (Alopecia) *i.e.*, patchy hair loss is a common disease all over the world, Hair is main part of personality and has always remained centre of attraction and everybody is extra conscious about hairs. In modern medicine, lot of remedies are available for 'Indralupta' (Alopecia) which are in the form of steroids with toxic side effects, skin irritant, less effective and recurrence of disease is common. The Hair transplantation is modern surgical management for Alopecia. But it is less effective and with post operative complication. So there are number of prescriptions and surgical treatment for Alopecia but still they have their own complications and limitations.

"Ayurvedic" medicine also has a number of prescription for "Indralupta" (Alopecia) one of which is used for this trial namely 'Romasanjanana Lepa' ('Karanja', 'Kasisa', 'Kasisa'). This 'Ayurvedic' remedies are economical without side effect and easily available in market. This preparation can be given on OPD (Out Patient Department) Basis and doesn't require hospitalisation. Thus patients can continue their routine work. The present study was undertaken to the concept of aetio–pathology of 'Indralupta' (Alopecia) and clinical co–relation on the 'Ayurvedic' Principles.

The present clinical study aims to evaluate the efficacy, specificity, limitations and scope of 'Ramasanjanana Lepa' in re–vitalising the growth of hair in 'Indralupta' (Alopecia).

Theoretical Co-relation of "Ayurvedic" and Modern Literature

An overview of aetiopathogenesis of "Indralupta" (Alopecia) indicated that major factor is derangement of 'Dosha', Pitta and Vata' which destroyed the hair follicle and hair fall occurs.

Along with above derangement 'Rakta and Kapha Dosha' blocks the opening of '*Romkupa*'. So further normal growth of hair becomes inhibited. According to modern view the aetiology of this disease is not yet known but may be of a nature of psycho–somatic disorder. So it is very difficult to co–relate "Ayurvedic" view with modern aetiopathology of patchy hair loss.

In modern science the aethiopathology of patchy hair loss is not specific but "Ayurveda" has mentioned much detailed and scientific aetiopathology about patchy hair loss.

General Observation

The maximum number of patients were of '*Madhyama Awastha*' (Middle age) *i.e.,* 17 to 40 age of their life, residing in urban area. Literate, Hindu, having personal habits like tea, coffee, tobacco were present. Near about equal history of gradual and sudden onset of the disease was present the occipital region was common site of disease 68 number of patches were found. Development period had history of started from very less period to onwards. The most common manifestation under this clinical study of "Indralupta" (Alopecia) patchy hair loss associated signs and symptoms exhibits Itching, Whitishness, Unctuousness, Roughness, Cleanness, dryness were found in majority of cases.

Effect of Cosmetic and Soaps on Scalp

Each and everyone is using soap on scalp in present series of study. Soap plays an important role in developing 'Indralupta' (Alopecia) than shampoo. In very few cases they had history of Typhoid, Psoriasis, pneumonia and pyoderma which were causative factors of developing "Indralupta" (Alopecia) in this study.

Role of Physical Examination

'Dehaprakriti (Doshika set–up) : In this study of 'Deha prakruti' (constitution of body) 'Pitta–Vata prakruti' patients were common and 'Vata–Kapha', 'Kapha–Pitta prakriti' patients were equally common in developing Alopecia. 'Prakriti' plays an important role in developing "Indralupta" (Alopecia).

Role of 'Nidan' (Aetiological Factor) in "Indralupta" (Alopecia)

Certain 'Nidan' (Aetiological factors) which are responsible for development of 'Alopecia' (Indralupta') must be avoided *'Apathykaraka–Ahar–Vihar'* (defective and harmful dietary habits and defective mode of living) and use of soaps (cosmetics) on scalp leads the formation of 'Alopecia' should be avoided. The identification of which has been considered to be of great diagnostic and Therapeutic significance specially in prevention of disease.

The concept of '*Apathyakar–Ahar,–Vihar*' in specially 'Pitta, Vaṭa prakriti' (constitution of body) from 'sthanik' (local) 'Dosha–Dusthi' (Derangement of 'Doshas') leads in development of '*Sthansansrya*' (Derangement of local tissue or site) and this derangement is responsible for defective functioning of hair follicle.

And this is basic approach to the early detection that means hair fall and stoppage. Use of cosmetics and soaps can be controlled by applying an appropriate treatment before the disease takes its full form.

Action of 'Romasanjanana Lepa' ("Ayurvedic" Concepts)

The ingredient of 'Romasanjanana Lepa' are 'Amla' (sour), 'Tikta' (bitter) 'Katu' (pungent), 'Kashaya' (astringent) 'Rasa' (taste) 'Ushna' and 'Shita virya' (hot and cooling effect) 'vata–kaphaghna' (Reduces deranged 'Vata' and 'Kapha') 'Rakta–Tridoshaghna' (Reduces deranged 'Rakta–Tridosha') in 'Doshaghnata' (Reduction of Deranged Dosha). They reduces deranged 'Kapha and '*Rakta Dhatu*' in '*Romkupa*' (hair follicle) and along with they also clear the derangement of 'Pitta' and 'Vata Dosha' resulting in further normal generation of hair.

Efficacy of 'Romasanjanana Lepa' in "Indralupta" (Alopecia)

It was observed that the trial preparation produces significant results and marked improvement in patients. Screening examination length of generated hair totally covered area of patches proved that the patient got totally cured.

It is concluded according to data presented in this thesis that the 'Romasanjanana Lepa' was significantly, effective in 'Alopecia' as well as hair loss caused by psoriasis, post–Typhoid, post pneumonia and post pyoderma diseases. None of the patient exhibited any toxic or side effects with the use of 'Romasanjanana Lepa'. No toxicity of drug was observed in local application of lepa. The result are assessed on the patients those who could be followed upon screening, hair measurement and symptomatic relief.

The preparation of 'Romasanjanana Lepa' being cheap, easy to prepare, effective, potent without side effect. The result of studies tabulated suggest that the 'Romasanjanana Lepa' of "*Ayurveda*" is best in patchy hair loss disease 'Indralupta' (Alopecia) where generation of hair is desired.

The Further Experimental Study is Planning to Observe the :

1. Clinical Study of the drug.
2. Drug Analysis :

   Physical Activity

   Chemical Activity

   Biological Activity

I. Physical Activity :

(*a*) PH.

(*b*) Ash–Acid insoluble.

Total Ash.

Water soluble.

Sp. Gravity.

Total Solids.

II. Chemical

(*a*) HPTLC activity ingredients as reference std.

(*b*) Total Alkaloids %

(*c*) Total Gycosides %

(*d*) Volatile oil/Essential Oil%

(*e*) Other Phyto-Chemical activity.

III. Biological Activity

3. Animal Study :

(*a*) Teratogenic effect of the drug.

(*b*) Mutogenic study of drug.

(*c*) Carcinogenic effect the drug.

To see the toxicity of drug ('Romasanjanana Lepa').

Case – 1

Before Treatment

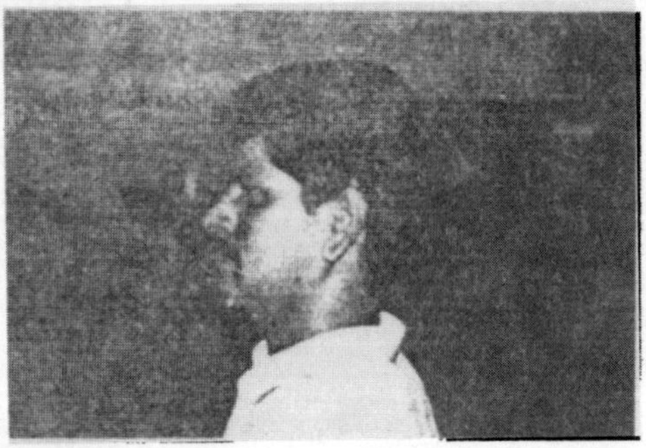

Case – 1

After Treatment

Case – 2

Before Treatment

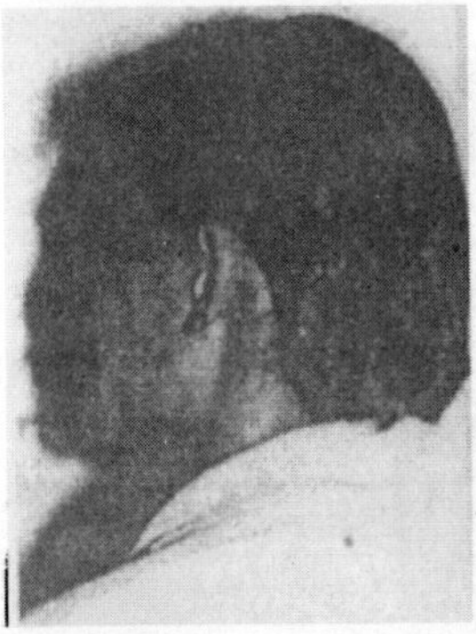

Case – 2
After Treatment

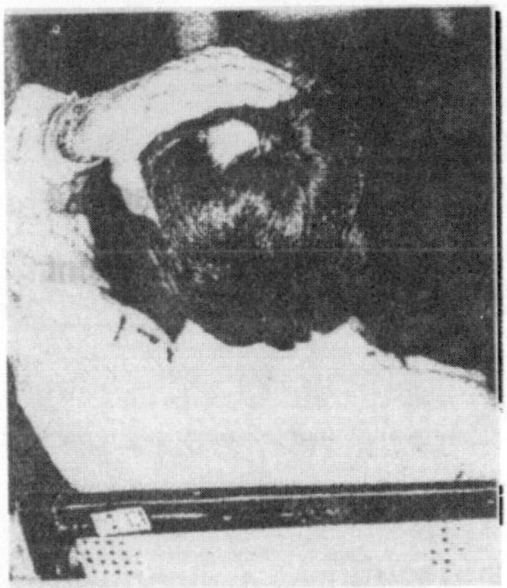

Case – 3
Before Treatment

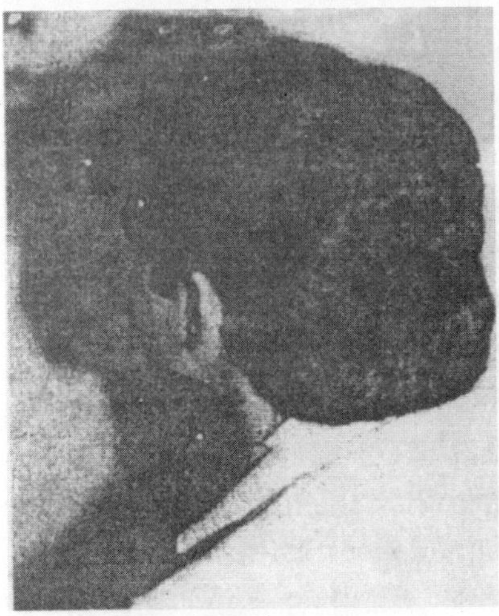

Case – 3
After Treatment

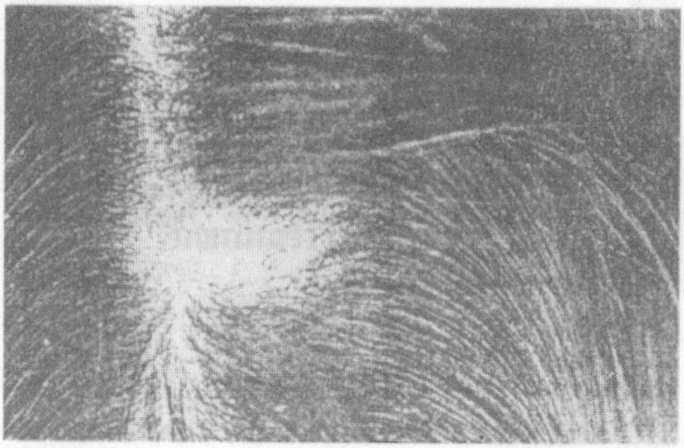

Case – 4
Before Treatment

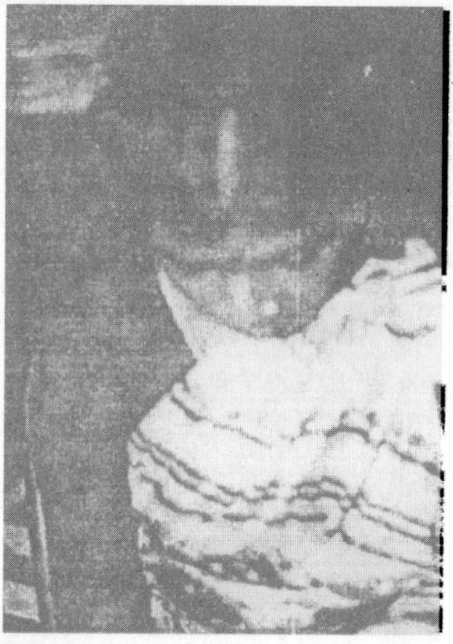

Case – 4
After Treatment

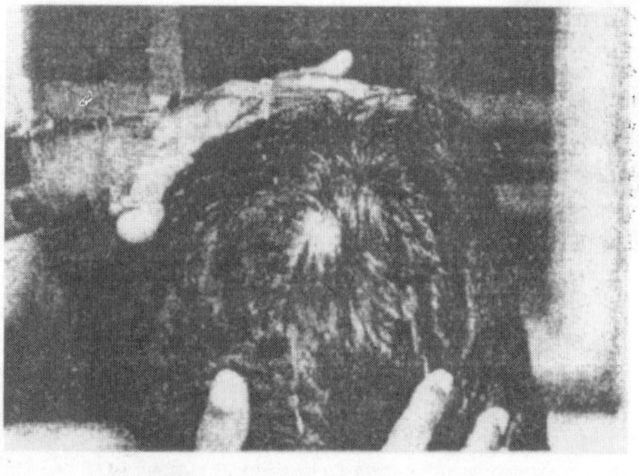

Case – 5
Before Treatment

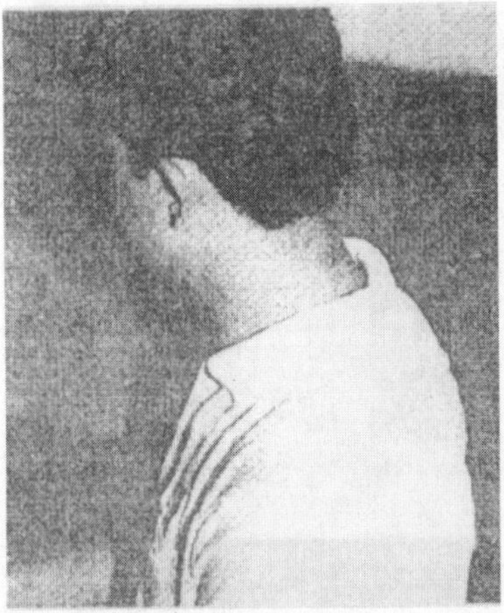

Case – 5

After Treatment

Case – 6

Before Treatment

Case – 7

After Treatment

KASIS

KAPITTHA

KARANJPATRA

CHAPTER 5

CLINICAL DIETETICS IN CHARAK SAMHITA WITH SPECIAL REFERENCE TO SKIN, SKIN CARE AND SKIN DISEASES

J.Y. Deopujari
Dhanvantaree Hospital, Khare Town,
Dharam Peth, Nagpur 10.
Prof. Dr. P.H. Kulkarni

Abstract

The general consideration and deitary advice regarding skin care, skin diseases and dietetics in Charak Samhita are based on long term observations. This paper is an attempt to highlight the same which will be helpful to clinicians while treating the skin diseases.

Key Words

Charak Samhita, Clinical dietetics, skin diseases, Skin Care, dietary advice.

Introduction

Due to the pollution and faulty way of life number of skin diseases are increasing day by day. The allergic manifestation of different food articles and other substances in day to day life is also of great concern in today medical practice.

Hypersensitivity to certain drugs and its skin manifestation is known to us. Rat race in day to day life and the resultant stress is contributing to skin diseases. Even with the advances in medicine dietary restrictions play an important role in the treatment of skin diseases. In food allergies, to find out the allergene and avoid it is the only effective treatment. Some skin diseases are haunting mankind since thousands of years and still there is no permanent remedy for these diseases like Psoriasis and eczema etc., in these diseases also diet may play an important role as a triggering factor or to keep the disease in inactive form.

On the other hand people are becoming beauty conscious and the herbal cosmetics are very popular all over the world. In this field also to maintain our natural beauty Ayurveda advised proper diet according to the constitution of an individual.

Aim

Even though the number of skin diseases is less in Ayurvedic texts when compared with the modern medicine, the dietary advice in Ayurvedic texts is based on the long term observation of the disease process. The aim of this paper is to highlight this wisdom in dietary advice specially related to skin diseases. The concept of skin and the dietary measures to keep skin healthy from Charak Samhita is also discussed in this paper so as to get some clues for further research in this field.

Limitations

This is an opinion paper based on Charak Samhita. We may get more information on this subject in some other compendiums. Skin diseases can be divided into two major groups, (*a*) only skin diseases and (*b*) the skin manifestation of some other systemic diseases. The information in this paper is confined only up to the group (*a*) as mentioned above.

The Concept of the Skin

The word "Twacha" means skin in derived from the word "Twacha Sauvarane" *i.e.*, the organ which covers the body from outside.[1] In Charak Samhita Twach *i.e.*, skin is defined as the organ which covers the body from outside.[2] "Twacha" is suppose to be originated from "Mansa Dhatu".[3]

Anatomically Charakacharya has described the six layers and the corresponding diseases of the skin. The outermost layer is "Udakadhara". The second one holds the blood. The third is the seat of Sidhma and Kilas Kushtha. The fourth layer is the seat of "Dadru kushtha". The fifth layer produces "Alaji" and "Vidradhi". The sixth and the deepest layer is the origin of red and black coloured boils and glands.[4]

Other than anatomical description we find the description of the natural texture of the skin in "Prakriti" and "Sara Parikshana" in Charak Samhita.

1. "Vata Prakriti"

In person belonging to this class the skin is dry (Ruksha), rough (Khara), cold (Sheeta) with less sweating (Alpasweda) or without sweating (Aswed) and its colour is black and smoky (Krishna and Dhoosara).[5]

2. "Pitta Prakriti"

In pitta Prakriti person the skin is hot (Ushna) secreates more sweat (Atiswed) and doesn't tolerate the heat. Different colour pigmentation is also present in this type of skin. Skin colour is fair and yellowish to yellow.[6]

3. *"Kapha Prakriti"*

In kapha Prakriti person the skin is unctuous (snigdha) soft (Mridu), and cold (sheeta) colour is fair whitish and very pleasant to see.[7]

4. *"Twak Sara Purush Lakshan"*

The skin is usually unctuous (Snigdha) smooth (shlakshna) soft (Mridu), very pleasant and with a luster over it.[8]

Even though the skin condition and other description of a single Prakriti is given in text, in practice we always get the combination of two or three Doshas in a single person. Sama Prakriti is also a rare condition. So in practice we label the prakriti according to the predominance of the Dosha as 'Vatakaphaj' or 'Pitta Vataj Prakriti' etc.

In Charak Samhita the Dosha and Rasa are interlinked on the basis of Panchamahabhoota theory.[9] So the dietary advice for each Dosha Prakriti is as follows. Because only Rasa are indicated, this format is applicable to all parts of the country. This can be modified as per Desh (geological considerations) and Ritu (Season).

1. Vata Prakriti–Beneficial Rasa–Snigdha (sour and Saline teste) Amla and Lavan[10].
2. Pitta Prakriti–Kashay (Astringent) Tikta (Bitter) and Mahur[10] (Sweet).
3. Kapha Prakriti–Katu (pungent) Tikta (Bitter) and Kashay[10] (Astringent).

We have, already discussed that we could not find single Doshik Prakriti in practice. So we have to finalised "Rasa" accordingly to the predominance of the Dosha.

This type of dietary advice syncronized with "Ritu Charya" is beneficial not only for skin but also to keep our body healthy and fit.

The Effect of "Rasa" on Skin

According to Charak Samhita the effect of food article on the body is predominantly due to its taste *i.e.,* "Rasa". Hence general effect of different "Rasa" on the body are also mentioned along with the properties of individual food articles. The "Rasa" also directly affects the "Dosha". Madhur rasa (Sweet) in general, increases the lustre of the skin. It is suppose to be beneficial for skin and hair.[11]

Amla Rasa (Sour) has no direct effect on the skin but if taken in excess can increase the process of pus formation in the preexisting injury or eruption on the skin.[12]

Lavan Rasa (Saline teste) if taken in excess can increase create cuts on the skin particularly in preexisting skin diseases. It accelerates the wrinkle formation on the skin and graying of hair as well as alopecia.[13]

Katu Rasa (Pungent) can reduce the oiliness as well as itching of the skin but at the same time can create patches over the skin.[14]

"Tikta Rasa" (Bitter) in general is useful in all skin diseases. It reduces almost all secretions in the body.[15]

"Kashaya Rasa" (Astringent) if taken in excess can produce the tanning over the skin.[16]

Diet as an Etiological Factor in Skin Diseases

1. **Dietetic Incompatibility *i.e.,* "Viruddhahara":** This is a peculiar Ayurvedic concept related to diet–diet interaction and is described in all most all

Ayurvedic compendiums. In general along with some other diseases the dietetic incompatibility can produce skin eruptions, Leucoderma and different types of dermatitis. The famous example of this is milk and fish. This combination if taken together can cause many skin diseases. Some other combinations are described in Charak Samhita at different places like, (*a*) Milk + Honey + Bamboo leaf + Badahar these four if taken together can adversely affect the luster and texture of the skin, (*b*) Raddish + Garlic Sahijan three varieties of oscimum sanctum (Arjak, Sumukh, Surasa) should not be taken along with because they can create some skin diseases.[17]

2. **The "Kushtha" and the food Articles :** Kushtha is the synonym for skin diseases in Ayurved. It is not only leprosy but all most all skin diseases are mentioned with this word. Though the full length description of todays skin diseases is not available in Charak Samhita, the general consideration are of clinical importance even in todays practice. Raba (Molases), Fish. Badhar, Raddish, Makoy (Faciolus aconitifolius) if taken in excess can cause skin diseases Hayanak (a type of grain), Yavak (a type of grain), Cheena (a type of grain), Vanakodo (a type of grain), Kodo (a type of grain) if taken either with milk or milk products or with 'Ber' (Zizyphus Jujuba), Kulthi (Dolicloses Biflorus), Udad (Phaseolus Radiatus) Teesi, Barre (Carthomus Tinclorius) and sneha (fats) if taken regularly or in excess can cause the skin diseases.[10]

3. According to Charak Samhita easily digestible food and the vegetable with Pungent taste are useful in

all skin diseases. The ghee prepared with Bhilava (Marking Nuts), Trifala (Three Myrobalans) and Nimba (Azadirechta Indica) if used along with food is also useful in skin diseases. Old grains, Jangal Mansa (Flesh of the animals belonging to dry land and forest), Moong (Phaseolus Mungo) Parvar ka Shak (Trichosanthes cucumerina) are also beneficial in skin diseases.[19]

Heavy diet, sour teste, curd, milk, Aanup Mansa (Flesh of the animals belonging to marshy land) Gud (Jaggari) Til (Sesamum) are contraindicated in all skin diseases.[20]

Conclusion

From the information mentioned above we can conclude that all most every aspect of dietary advice to skin care and diseases are discussed in Charak Samhita and on the basis of this we can rewrite the dietary regime applicable in todays life.

REFERENCES

1. Shabda Kalpadruma.
2. Ayurved Shabdakosh.
3. Cha. Sharir 7/4.
4. Ch. Chiki 15/16–17.
5. Ch. Viman 8/98.
6. Ch. Viman 8/97.
7. Ch. Viman 8/96.
8. Ch. Viman 8/103.
9. Ch. Sutra 1/64.
10. Ch. Viman 1/6, Ch. Viman 1/66.
11. Ch. Sutra 26/43–1.

12. Ch. Sutra 26/43–2.
13. Ch. Sutra 26/43–3.
14. Ch. Sutra 26/43–4.
15. Ch. Sutra 26/43–5.
16. Ch. Sutra 26/43–6.
17. Ch. Sutra 26/84.
18. Ch. Nidan 5/6.
19. Ch. Chiki 7/820.
20. Ch. Chiki 7/83.

CHAPTER 6

REDISCOVERING SUCHI KARMA

Dr. Frank Ros
Adelaide, Australia,
Australasian Academy of Natural Medicine
Ayurvedic Faculty, Australia.

Many of the ancient therapeutic concepts in India are once again making a powerful comeback into mainstream Indian society, after hundreds of years of neglect and almost total annihilation. Interestingly, these concept are likewise making huge inroads into Western society and becoming a major part of the countries health fabric in the West.

Suchi Karma, literally "needle therapy" is well–known to have been practised in India for thousands of years.[1] A number of ancient acupuncture needles (suchi) have been recently excavated in Taxilla university site[2] and many scholars believe Suchi Karma to have started as a modification of Ayurveda on the icy slopes of the Himalayas, where it is difficult for herbs to grow.[3] Ayurvedic acupuncture has been in use in Northern India and Sri Lanka for thousands of years.[4]

Suchi Karma is the Indian type of acupuncture where a specialised needle, a *suchi* is used to pierce the skin at a location called *marma;* the junction of a number of different types of tissues (*e.g.*, bones, flesh, arteries, nerves, and joints) where there is also a lower galvanic resistance than surrounding areas of the body. These marmas or vital points have been utilised in Indian martial arts and Ayurvedic surgery for thousands of years and are needled because they connect with internal organs (*e.g.*, the liver) via specialised channels of bio–energy. Most marmas can be needled (there are some exceptions) as minute, gentle trauma produced by the needle can stimulate the body into repair just as a homeopathy, Suchi Karma works on the energetic system of the body to facilitate health. Prana is the bio–energy which travels through the channels (*nadis*) and affects the function of the organs by providing balance to them. These energy channels vitalise the marmas. In so doing, the three doshas or Ayurvedic humoural energies are likewise affected as each organ in the human body is related to one of these three humour (Tridoshas).

By needling the appropriate marmas, Tridoshas can be balanced, allowing the organs their proper function, that is to work in harmony with each other. The Tridoshas are simply three orientations of Prana, the life force. They maintain balance in the body by ensuring that the person is neither too hot or too cold, too moist or too dry. Their vitiation results in the development of disease. A disease, being an imbalance in these body functions can be eliminated by needling as its purpose is to "*stimulate, repair and heal these vital points through Ayurvedic acupuncture*"[5] There are a multitude of marmas on the body but 360 are recognised as important, with 107 classified as having lethal effects if injury occurs to these. Just like the 360 degree in a circle, the marmas are like pearls in a necklace, with the nadis or channels being the thread. The nadis or Pranic channels from a type of loop or circle linking the organs and marmas together.

In order to treat dermatological disorders with Suchi Karma, a through diagnosis of the affected Dosha or humour must be undertaken as well as the unbalanced related organs. For instance, if the dermal symptoms involve Pitta (inflammation, rashes etc.) marmas or points on the liver channel (*Yakrit Nadi*) may need to be treated in order to calm Pitta and balance the liver, since it is a Pitta–related organ. In cases where Vata is vitiated in dermal disorders (*e.g.*, dryness, itchiness), the Large Intestine channel (*Sthulantra Nadi*) may primarily need to be treated as the large intestine is an organ directly related to Vata. Kapha type skin disorder (*e.g.*, weeping dermal eruptions, swelling, paleness of skin) may require treatment of the stomach Channel (*Amashaya Nadi*) (or its related Spleen channel *Pliha Nadi*) as the stomach is related to Kapha, being its primary site. Vital Points (marmas) along other channels may also require treatment according to well–established connections and protocols between certain organs and their related humoural energies (Vata, Pitta or Kapha).

There are certain points which have specific reactions which may likewise be required in treatment. For instance, in the event that Jathara Agni (digestive small intestine fire) is weak, the *Indrabasti Marmas* may be needled, Indrabasti is found on the leg, at the junction between the belly of gastrocnemius and the Achilles' tendon (*Pada Indrabasti*). It is also found about half way along the forearm, in the centre of the outside of the arm. Where a hormonal imbalance may also be present, *Amsa Marma,* midway between the spine and acromial angle, on the rear of the torso may be needled also as this is the major endocrinal and thyroid gland marma.

In dermatological disorders one vital point can not be overlooked, as clinical experience has shown its importance in the treatment of skin disorders, especially in dermatitis and eczema. This marma or vital print located on the top part of the ear, that is one the apex of the ear (Karna) is called the dermal/allergy point.[6] This point has also proved therapeutically brilliant in cases where the immune system has been suppressed and allergies have become evident.

The *Adhipati Marma* located in the crown, on top of the head is a major needling point for most disorders including dermatological ones. *Adhipati means* "Overlord" emphasizing this point's importance in **administering and controlling** of most body/mind functions. Adhipati marma is located along the *Amatya Nadi* (Minister channel) which itself has an extremely important function, that is to 'minister' over all nadis (channels) and marmas (vital points), since amatya means "minister". Adhipati marma produces an incredibly relaxed state in the patient when needled, a very important requirement for health and therapy.

Suchi karma otherwise also called Ayurvedic acupuncture can not only be used to treat established chronic disorders, but also in acute conditions. As with Ayurveda, Suchi karma is wholistic and first and foremost preventative where a person may receive a treatment in order to retain health and not just when there is an established disease or obvious symptoms. Suchi Karma though is not a panacea for all ills, but clinical results clearly demonstrates its usefulness in a wide range of conditions and as a very important adjunct to the Ayurvedic practitioner.

For further references and information on Suchi Karma, the reader is directed to *The Lost Secrets of Ayurvedic Acupuncture by* Dr. Frank Ros, Lotus Publications U.S.A. (1994). Also Published in several other languages including German (Windpferd Verslagsgesellschaft mbH) and Italian

(Edizioni Ilpunto D'incontro) and also in India (Motilal Banarsidass Publ.).

REFERENCES

1. Wexu, M. Modern Guide to Ear Acupuncture. Dr. C. Thakkur. Aurora press, N.M.USA 1985. p. 187.
2. Nagpal, D.L. Modern Acupuncture, I.Ac.T.R.I. Publishers, Jaipur, India, p. 4.
3. Jayasuriya, A. Clinical Acupuncture. B. Jain Publishers, New Delhi. India. Seventh Edition. p. 369.
4. Ibid., p. 17.
5. Tiwari, M. Ayurveda Secrets of Healing. Lotus Publications, Twin Lakes, USA 1995. p. 92.
6. Wexu, M. Modern Guide to Ear Acupuncture. Dr. C. Thakkur. Aurora Press, N.M. USA 1985. p. 186.

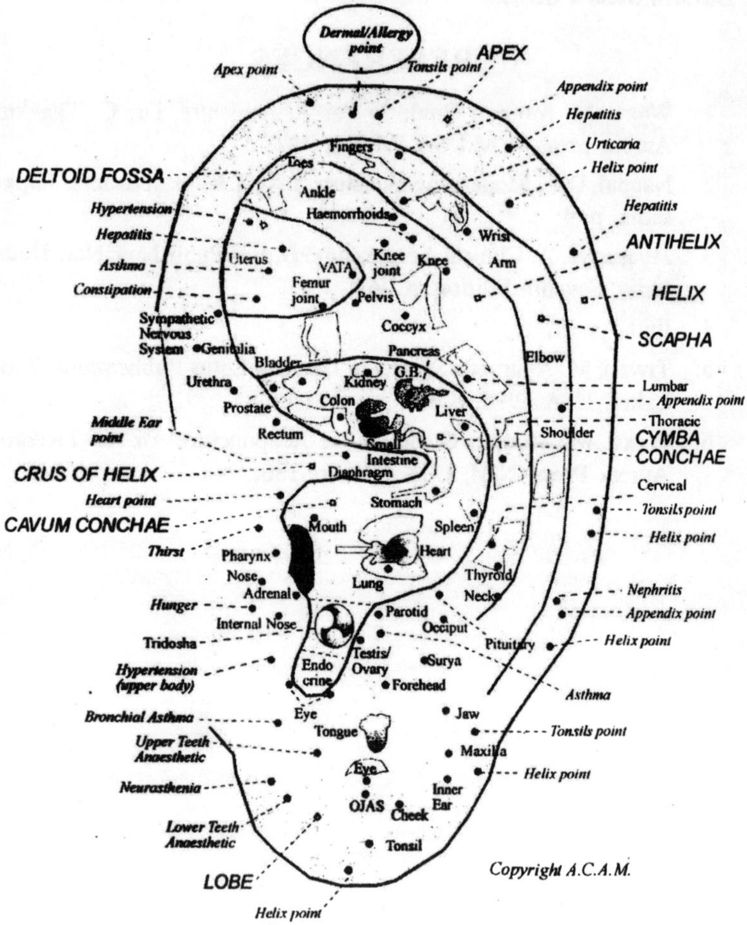

Ayurvedic Acupuncture
CHART OF THE EAR POINTS

CHAPTER 7

HERBAL SKIN–REJUVENATIVES

Dr. Prakash Paranjape
Clinical Research Associate,
Ayurveda Research Institute, Pune.

Ayurveda means "The Science of Life". It does not mean Hindu medicine, nor must its herbalism be considered Indian herbalism. It is a science of living that encompasses the whole of life, and which relates the life of the individual to that of the universe. As such it is open to and includes all life, and all methods that bring us into greater harmony with life.

Life forms are stations for the reception and transmission of forces, through which all are nourished. Each thing exists to nourish all others, and, in turn, to be nourished itself. In this manner each kingdom of nature serves to receive and transmit life. The life is implicit in light and in the transmission of stellar or astral forces.

The earth, like a gigantic receptor, inhales and exhales stellar and cosmic forces, the absorbed essence of which grows and unfolds as life. These forces are not all material, but includes subtle energies of an occult or spiritual nature. Plants transmit the vital–emotional impulses, the life force that is hidden in life. That is the gift, the grace, the power of plants.

Plants exists to transmute light into life. Human being exists to transmute life into consciousness, love. These three light, life and love–are one, each an expression of the other three dimensions of same existence. The plants transmute light into life through photosynthesis. The human being transmute life into consciousness through perception. Through direct perception. The seer is the seen. The observer the observed. The Sanskrit word for the plant Ousadhi means literally a receptacle or mind, dhl, in which there is burning transformation, osa. In the Vedas this can mean not only plants but all entitles in creation. In order to understand the Ayurvedic approach to herbs, one must understand the basic system of Ayurveda, which is a complete healing science, including the physical, psychological and spiritual aspects of life.

Ayurvedic herbology reaches its culmination in the science of rejuvenation. Aimed at renewal of both body and mind, Ayurvedic herbology does not seek simply longevity, but moves towards a life of pure awareness, natural creativity, spontaneous delight. The approach is not only towards physical immortality, but the immortality of mind, the daily renewal of brain cells. This science is called as 'Rasayan'. Rasayan is what enters (ayana), in the essence (rasa). It is what penetrates and revitalizes the essence of our psycho-social being.

Rasayana substances (rejuvenatives) rebuild the body–mind, prevent decay, and postpone ageing. They may even reverse the ageing process. They do not simply add to the bulk or quantity of the body, but augment its quality. Rasayana substances are more subtle, more specific and more lasting than more nutritive tonics. Their action sustains the optimal form and functions of the various organs, dhatus and doshas in the body.

In ancient scriptures of Ayurveda, Vegbhatta acclaims that rasayana endows longevity, memory, health, intelligence, youth, voice, skin complexion, energy, sexual vitality and beauty. (Vagbhatta, Uttrasthana, 39/1–2). The rasayana substance is commonly used to improve the energy levels of normal individual, to prevent premature ageing and alleviate the disease. Charaka also had adulated about rasayana as Vagbhatta had. Chakrapani has mentioned rasayana to be the superior one to vajikara and has praised as Mahaphala more benevolent.

The substances, usually used as medicines, to combat the disease are many a times hard, sharp and subtle, to accord quicker effects. Hence, they are prepared from vyavayi and vikasi or even toxic substances to achieve quicker dosha: shamana or vedana shamana etc. Though effective, they may cause ill effects on dhatus. Rasayanas, on the contrary, many a times used are mild either or given along with ghrita, milk etc. They can be used in any age are unlike vajikar aphrodisiacs. The concept of rasayana is used since centuries in India, right from Veda periods. The famous story of seer Chyavana is known since ages.

The mode of action of a rasayana is said to be on tissues (dhatugat Parivartana) directly, on various systems in the body by augmenting their immunity (vyadhikshamatvagata parivartana) and all endocrinal secretions (antasravagata parivartana). Maharshi charaka has enlisted specific rasayanas on all specific dhatus–tissues, and also on specific srotasas systems. It is mentioned that Shatavari (Asparagus racemosus) and Bala (Sida cordifolia) for rasa–dhatu; Lohadi rasayana for rakta–dhatu, Ashwagandha (Withania somnifera), Shatavari (Asparagus racemosus), Nagabala (Grewia thirsuta), Kushmanda (Benincasa hispida) for asthi–dhatu, medhya rasayana meda–dhatu, Ajasthi and Praval (coral) for asthi–dhatu, medhya rasayana for majja–dhatu *viz.*, Brahmi (Bacopa monniera), Shankhapushpi (convolvulus pluricaulis), vrishya–yoga for shukra–dhatu and Amalaki (Phyllanthus emblica) rasayana as all dhatu rasayana.

The rasayana for the skin, will be basically a rasayana for rasa and rakta dhatu. The correlation of the skin with these dhatus is well established even clinically. Along with these two doshas, one should also take account of mamsa dhatu and doshas, especially, pitta. These all, are interrelated with the metabolism and the health of the skin. The rasayanas for the skin work well, both topically as well as systemically. Innumerable herbs have been mentioned in ancient scriptures of Ayurveda which impart a rejuvenative activity on the skin.

The most commonly used herbs, which possed a rasayana actions on the skin, can be mentioned as Guduchi (Tinospora cordifolia), Daruharidra (Berberis aristata), Brahmi (Bacopa Monniera), Amalaki, (Phyllanthus emblica), Yashtimadhu (Glycyrrhiza glabra), Haritaki (Terminalia chebula), Guggulu (commiphora mukul), Bhringaraj (Eclipta alba), Bibhitaka (Terminilia belerica), Priyangu (Callicarpa acrophylla) and so on. It will be quite interesting to study how they act on the skin. Majority of the herbs impart blood purifying action (raktashodhaka), cooling properly (dahaprashamana), detoxification (amanashaka), hepatobiliary stimulant action (yakrutottejaka, pitta sransana, anulomana etc.), cleansing kleda shoshana), augment metabolic fire (agnideepan), astringent (stamphana), antimicrobial (krimighna), antihistaminic (Kandughna) action.

In day to day practice, there are number of herbs used, though they may not be categorised under rasayana herbs but are used with benefit. These are nimba (Azadirachta indica), manjishtha (Rubia cordifolia), khadira (Acacia catechu), Jatamansi (Nardostachys Jatamansi), haridra (Curcuma longa), sariva (Hemidesmus indicus), vidanga (embelia ribes), raktachandan (Pterocarpus santalinus), bakuchi (Psoralia corylifolia) and so many. They are umpteen formulations in Ayurveda, as skin rejuvenatives, topical as well as systemic, which impart excellent results on their long term use. They cure and alleviate the pigment disorders, allergic manifestations of the skin, rashes, swellings, dryness, wrinkling, skin diseases, ulcers and bestow a fair complexion and a glow to the skin.

The rejuvenators create a perfect balance and harmony in doshas, dhatus and even malas. Though the rejuvenators specifically recommended for specific dhatus, their role is not merely restricted. All the dhatus, when are in their normal condition, the semen or reproductive tissue is the essence of all bodily tissues and contains within itself not only the power of reproduction, but also that of rejuvenation. The essence of the semen the cream of the body, is called ojas, which means "that which invigorates". Ojas is thus the essence of the body, the substance of all hormonal secretions, and supports, the auto–immune system. Ayurveda, our ancient wisdom, categorizes herbs according to the dhatus or tissues upon which they work, the doshas in which they maintain harmony and create balance. Herbal skin rejuvenatives in reality are not the rejuvenatives to the skin alone, but are the panacea for physical, psychological and spiritual well–being of an individual in a true wholistic sense.

CHAPTER 8

CLINICAL ASSESSMENT OF EFFICACY OF AYURVEDIC OILS IN THE FORM OF CREAMS

Prof. Dr. P.H. Kulkarni
Director, Institute of India Medicine,
Research Guide University of Pune
36, Kothrud, Pune 4411029 (India)

Ayurvedic medicated oils are used as BAHYOPACHAR (External treatment) in many diseases as single treatment or adjuvant to other therapy. Skin is covering of human body and is better route for administering any medicine.

We selected five oils Manufactured by Ayurvedic Rasashala, Pune 411004, for preparing creams. (1) Narayan Oil, Vishagrabha oil (2) Paribhadra oil. (3) Chandanbala lakshadi oil, (4) Vranropak oil, (5) Bavachi tail and Nimb tail (Nimba oil from another manufacturer).

Why in The Form of Cream

Oils are–sticky, difficult to apply without external help (*e.g.,* One's back). On the other hand–Creams are:

1. Easy to apply.
2. Easy to handle.
3. Independence in self application.

4. Ph– could be maintained–Non irritant to skin.
5. Economic–Since wastage is minimum.
6. Pleasant while application and afterwards also.
7. Acceptable appearance.

More penetrating than thick oils, no cloth staining, no disagreeable smell, Oil can not be applied by self.

Creams were prepared 10% to 20%. It is observed that creams containing more than 20% oil comes out after 2 weeks. Hence finally fixed at 15%. Distributed for trails in India and abroad. Experienced by doctors and research workers. It is reported that creams are effective, no side effects and well accepted.

$$\text{Base}: \frac{\text{Wax/Bees Wax}}{\text{25 Castor Oil}} + \text{LANOLIN} + \underset{\text{Other Oils}}{(\text{TRO})} + 50\%\ \text{Water}$$

Oil Depends on Applications Of

Cream : Easy penetration, oil slips on skin, Viscosity control, cream remains, Ph can be estimated.

1. Bavachi Nimba Cream (Vanishing Cream Base) Useful in Leucoderma (Vitilgo) and Dermatitis of any origin.

   Tried in India and Australia with good results.

2. C.B. Cream Chandanbala Lakshadi tail (oil) Vanishing cream base. Ideal cream for massage. Advised in Paralysis, paresis Poliomylitis etc. Useful for skin care.

   V.D. Agte case, tried in India, Australia, New Zealand, good results.

3. N.V. Cream (Narayan Tail Oil) + Vishgarbha Tail (Oil) Vanishing creams base. Most useful in joint

pain and or muscular pain, increases muscle tone advocated for massage.

Tried in Yoga School of Hungery, West Germany, Australia, New Zealand, Patients in India and other countries.

4. V.R. Creams (Vraṇaropak Tail) (Oil) Vanishing Cream base useful for natural healing of any kind of wounds, ulcers etc.

   Dr. Parchure's diabetic patient Dr. B.J. Naik's diabetic patients. Adelaide case avoided amputation.

5. P.B. Cream

   Psoriasis cream used in Australia.

Acknowledgement

Thanks are due to Ayurved Rasashala, Pune–411 004. Shri, Gangal of Melisa Herbals, Panvel.

CHAPTER 9

CLINICAL ASSESSMENT OF THIOSTANIN IN SKIN DISORDERS

Prof. Dr. B.B. Date & Prof. Dr. P.H. Kulkarni
Institute of Indian Medicine,
36, Kothrud, Pune 411 029

Introduction

Thiostanin is one of the specialities of Ayurved Rasashala, Pune 4. It is indicated in variety of skin diseases. In this research project, I have made an attempt to assess the efficacy of the drug on various skin conditions which are pathological. I have treated patients having different skin disorders with either Thiostanin alone or Thiostanin internally and Paribhadra Taila, which is specific Oil preparation externally.

Composition

A. Each 250 mg. tablet of Thiostanin represents.

1. Gandhka (Shudda) *i.e.*, purified sulphur 110 mgs.
2. Vangabhasma *i.e.*, incinerated ash of Tin (Stannum) 80 mg.
3. Kajjali *i.e.*, well triturated combination of mercury and sulphur (both purified 4 mgs.)

Other ingredients are incinerated ashes of Loha (Iron), Abhraka (Mica), Tamra (Copper), Triphala (Three myrobalans), Shilajatu (Asphaltum), Guggulu (Commiphore mukul), Chitraka (P. Zeylanica), Katuka (Picrokrhiza Kurrao), and Guduchi (T Cardifolia)

B. Composition of Parbhandra Taila

Oil of sesame is processed or treated with juice of Neem-leaves (leaves of Azadirachta indica) by boiling until water content is evaporated off.

Methodology

(*i*) As it was general assessment of efficacy of Thiostanin alone on various skin diseases in patients of Gr. A. and assessment of efficacy of Thiostanin (internally) and Paribhadra Oil (externally) used together in patients of Gr. B. The assessment was clinical only. Dose of Thiostanin was 2 tabs. tds. Paribhadra oil was to be applied to diseased skin portion to reduce itching.

(*ii*) Prakruti (Constitution) from Ayurved point of view, was noted to see the relation between the constitution, disease and efficacy of the drug.

(*iii*) Age, sex, occupation, education, cultural and financial status of Pts. were also noted.

(*iv*) Pts. were also instructed about the beneficial (Pathya) and harmful (Apathya) diet and behaviour.

(*v*) Pts. were treated for 60 days and check ups were carried on every fortnight.

Observations

(*i*) Thiostanin tablets are useful in pts., who have kaphapradhan pitta Constitution.

(*ii*) Thiostanin is useful in skin diseases, where Pitta and Kapha doshas are predominant.

(*iii*) In Vatapitta constitution pts. and in vatapitta skin diseases Thiostanin had no effect.

(*iv*) Thiostanin is useful comparatively in kaphapittaja or Pittakaphaja skin disorders which are acute rather than chronic.

(*v*) In chronic skin disorders 60 days treatment is not enough.

(*vi*) In skin disorders where itching is a prominent system the effect of external application of Paribhadra Oil, to the disease site is noteworthy. In such conditions Paribhadra oil is a good adjuvant to Thiostanin.

(*vii*) Those pts. who underwent Thiostanin treatment with or without Paribhadra oil, and observed the observances (pathyas) and restraints (Apathyas) exhibited better results than those who didn't or couldn't following them.

(*viii*) Thiostanin proved its efficacy prominently in pts. suffering from Eczema, Scabies, Ring worm and Nonspecific dermatitises. Especially in those cases where itching and oozing (wet condition) were prominently seen.

(*ix*) 6 out of 9 cases of Eczema, 2 cases out of 2 cases of Scabies, 2 cases out of 2 cases of ring worm and 1 case out of 2 cases of Nonspecific Dermatities responded very well to thiostanin. The pts recovered well, were found to observe the Do's and Don'ts as per advice and to take the medicines punctually, regularly and without break.

(*x*) 2 out of 5 cases of Pimples responded quite satisfactorily to Thiostanin. 1 out of 3 cases of Tinea Versicolor (Shibe) shows quite satisfactory response to Thiostanin. It was found that all these pts. had Kaphapitta as predominant doshas in their constitution.

(*xi*) Cases of Vitiligo and Allegeric Dermatitis did not at all respond to Thiostanin treatment.

(*xii*) Majority of the cases were Eczema and then of pimples and vitiligo.

(*xiii*) Majority of the patients were of Vatapitta or Pittavata constitutions. So Pitta Doshas was common in all the patients.

(*xiv*) Majority of the pts. (about 60%) were students and housewives.

(*xv*) Majority of the pts. (60%) were from lower middle class.

(*xvi*) It was surprising to find that 80% of the pts. were educated and cultured.

(*xvii*) Pts. having 'Kapha pradhan constitution' and having 'Kaphaja signs' responded very well to the Thiostanin and in comparatively short time.

(*xviii*) Unclean habits, irregularities in daily routine (in short avoiding the Dos and observing the Don'ts) consuming foods and drinks which are intolerable and troublesome to one's specific constitution and breaking the basic rules of health every now and then are the common causes seen creating etiological background to the skin disorders.

(*xix*) Mental tensions and stresses and emotional upsets were found in most of the pts.

(*xx*) Indigestion and constipation were found in most of the cases.

CHAPTER 10

COMPARATIVE EFFICACY OF FOUR AYURVEDIC FORMULATIONS IN THE TREATMENT OF ACNE VULGARIS : A DOUBLE BLIND RANDOMISED PLACEBO CONTROLLED CLINICAL EVALUATION

Dr. Prakash Paranjape &
Prof. Dr. P.H. Kulkarni

Summary

Eighty two patients with acne were randomised into five groups. Ayurvedic treatments were given orally for 6 weeks, while one group received placebo. Physical and clinical investigations were carried out at regular weekly intervals. A significant reduction in lesion count was observed in patients receiving Sundervati when compared with other Ayurvedic formulations, which failed to produce any significant difference from the pretreatment condition. The drug therapies were well tolerated.

Introduction

Acne vulgaris, a chronic inflammatory disorder of the pilosebaclous follicles, is an important disorder for which medical treatment is commonly sought in the clinical practice. It is major cause for both psychological and social disability and the rate of unemployment amongst young adults with acne is significantly higher in both males and females (Mostley and Finlay 1989, Cunliffe 1986). Treating acne has become a problem since safe drugs are not available for long term therapy. Systematic and tropical antibiotics have been used for long time though they are not completely free from adverse effects. The use of clindamycin may cause psuedomembranous colitis (Milstene *et. al.* 1981), tetracycline may colour the skin yellow and erythromycin may precipitate hepatic disorders (Coskey 1975). Though effective, Isotretinoin causes untoward effects with great frequency including risk ofteratogenicity (Lammer *et. al.* 1985). There is a clear need for a safer drug for long term therapy of acne vulgaris.

Ayurveda is the ancient science of life. In the Sanskrit language, "Ayu" means life and 'Veda' means knowledge. This brane of medicine has a very old record of use in the Indian system of medicine (Paranjpe, 1990) Charak Samhita, an Ayurvedic classic describes acne vulgaris as "Tarunya Peetika" meaning a disease of adolescence. A variety of drugs have used in the Ayurvedic system of medicine to treat this condition. These agents are Sookshma Triphala, Thiostanin, Amalakimashi Vati, Shankhabhasma Vaati and Sunder Vati and are claimed to be safe and effective (Sharangadhara Samhita 1984) but their effectiveness have not been tested in controlled clinical trials. Therefore we undertook a randomised, double blind placebo controlled clinical trial of these agents in the treatment of acne vulgaris.

Materials and Methods

Ayurvedic Medicines

Compositions of the four formulations are detailed in Table 1 and were obtained from the well-established company of ayurveda Rasashala of Pune which has a valid drug licence issued by the Government. The authenticity of each plant and mineral component was established by the quality control Laboratory of the Company by qualified chemist approved by the Food and Drug Administration. The fair formulations and the placebo were indistinguishable from each other on appearance taste and weight.

Clinical Studies

Forty male and forty two female patients between the ages of 18 and 28 years with moderate facial acne were recruited at Nanal hospital, Pune. Patients were selected on the basis of having moderate acne vulgaris of the face manifested by at least 10 papules or pustules and atleast 5 open or closed comedones. Patients with known hypersensitivity to drugs and those contemplating pregnancy were not admitted to the trial. At the time of entry into the study, they were in good health and biochemically eughyroid and non-diabetic. None of them had any endocrinal disorder. All topical and systemic acne treatment and medications, if any, were discontinued atleast two weeks before entry into the study. Their characteristics on entry are recorded in Table 2. During the study period patients were forbidden from taking any other medicaments and no instructions were given to the patients concerning the diet and the mechanical removal of comedones. Written informed consent and a detailed clinical history was obtained from the patients. They were randomised into five groups and the patients group did not differ significantly with regard to sex, age, diet, smoking status etc. In addition, the group did not differ widely in types of complexions, use of makeup, history of allergies and status of acne at the beginning of the study.

Dosage and Care Regimen

Medication was taken orally two tablets 3 times daily on arising, at the afternoon and at bed time. They first washed with mild soap and rinsed and patted their faces dry. The treatment was continued for six weeks.

Clinical Evaluation

The patients attended for clinical evaluation every two weeks and this was performed by one of the investigator to help to assure constancy of evaluation. Two types of evaluations were made.

1. The exact number of each lesion type present on the face from ear to ear and above the mandibular line was counted separately for each side of the face and the counts for each side was then summed up.
2. For visits after the first examination, a clinical evaluation of patients overall change in facial acne compared with his or her appearance at the beginning of the study was then made on 5 point scale ranging from excellent to worst. The clinical evaluator was unaware of the treatment agent assigned to any subject. At each examination, the observer made sure that the patients were in any type of make–up that would obscure lesions and then counted each type of lesions Papula, pustule, nodulo cystic lesions, open or closed comedown.) For the purpose of analysis papules and closed comedones were combined as non–inflammatory lesions (Allen and smith, 1982). The patient's compliance was assessed by them every two weeks. Facial photographs were taken initially and at the end of the study.

Data Analysis

Statistical analysis of lesions count was performed on raw scores employing an analysis of variance (Anova) for repeated measures to assess change in each patient group over six weeks treatment period Demographic data and over response data were analysed by non–parametric X2 analysis.

Results

Sixty six patients completed the study and there were sixteen drop outs during the course of the study. The patients dropouts were due to various reasons including not getting benefit, domestic reasons and family problems (Table 3). The findings for changes in the total number of inflammatory lesions are summarised in Table 4. The drug group did not differ significantly before treatment for the lesions in this category. Treatment with Sundervati (Group 5) was associated with significant reduction (P 0.01) in lesion count of approximately 60 percent by the end of the treatment period. There was a significant reduction the total number of inflammatory lesions within 2 weeks reduction in the total number of inflammatory lesions within 2 weeks with further education at each observation period during six weeks treatment. The findings for change in the total number of non-inflammatory lesions are given in Table 5. Initial lesions counts were comparable in all the treatment groups. Treatment with Sundervati (Group 5) was associated with significant reduction in this lesion category. The overall percentage reductions (approximately 40) however were less than those seen with inflammatory lesions. As far as overall change in facial acne condition is concerned, the treatment in group 5 showed excellent response (Fig. 1 and Fig. 2) Nearly 2/3 of patients in this group had good to excellent clinical response by the end of the study period. Treatment in the other groups failed to produce any significant difference compared to the baseline values. The drug therapy in all the groups was well tolerated (Table No. 3).

Discussion

In the present study, ayurvedic drugs were given to unselected group of acne vulgaris patients. Treatment with Sundervati showed a significant improvement in the serverity of both inflammatory as well as non–inflammatory lesions. It appears that treatment with this ayurvedic formulation reduces the severity of acne and produces a clinically significant improvement in the severity of acne. However treatment with other ayurvedic formulation failed to show any significant clinical improvement. The response to treatment with Sundervati in this study is comparable to the results reported from other well controlled trails using ambitions and other agents (Dobson and Belknap 1980, Strauss *et. al.* 1984, Melski and Arndt 1980). The treatment did not produce any significant changes in other clinical parameters like pulse rate, body temperature etc. The exact mechanism of action of this novel Ayurvedic formulation cannot be documented from our study. Phyllanthus emblica is rich in Vitamin C (Chopra *et. al.* 1982) and may have immunomodulatory activity. Embelia ribes (Vidgana) is a common medicine used in Indian household and its aqueous extract has been shown to have antibacterial activity against staphylococcus aureus and E. coil (Chopra *et. al.,* 1982). Holarrhena antidysenterica (Kutajbark) has anstringent activity (Nadkarni 1975). Zingiber officinale (Sunth) has two terpenes, d–camphere and B phellandrene, and is reported to have anti–inflamatory activity (Chopra *et. al.* 1982). Whether this drug has any antiseptic and or anti inflammatory activity remains to be investigated. Further work is very much needed to investigate the long term effects and efficacy of this formulation.

Acknowledgement

We thank Dr. Pralhad Patki for protocol and design of this clinical trial. Cooperation from the management of Nanal Hospital Pune deserves special thanks.

REFERENCES

1. Allen B.S. and Smith J.G. (1982) Various parameters for granding acne. Archieves Dermatology 118, 23–25.
2. Charak Samhita (1949), Translated by Shree Gulabkunverba Ayurvedic Society, Jamnagar, India P. 5.
3. Chopra R.N. Chopra I.C., Handa K.L. and Kapur L.D. (1982) Indigenous drugs of India. Academic Publishers Calcutta. P. 673–684.
4. Coskey R.J. (1975). Side effects of antibiotics therapy in acne vulgaris, Cutis 15, 710–712.
5. Cunliffe W.J. (1986) Acne and unemployment. British Journal of Dermatology 115, 386–388.
6. Dobson RL and Belknap B.S. (1980). Topical therapy for acne New England Journal of Medicine 302, 503–506.
7. Lammer E.J. (1985). Retinesic and embryopathy. New England Journal of Medicine 313, 837–841.
8. Malski J.W. and Arndt K.A. (1980). Topical therapy for acne, New England Journal of Medicine 302, 503–156.
9. Milstone E.B. MC Donaid A.J., Scholhamer C.F. (1981). Practical use of disability index in the routine management of acne. British Journal of Dermatology 123. (Supplement 37) 21–22.
10. Nadkarni K.M. (1976). Indian Maleria Medica, Popular, Prakshan, Bombay P. 636.
11. Paranjape P., Patki P., Patwardhan B. (1990). Ayurvedic treatment of obesity : A randomised double blined palcebo–controlled clinical trial. Journal of Ethnopharmacology 29, 1–11.
12. Sharangdhar Samhita (1984). Translated by K.K. Shrikanta Murti, Chaukhamba Orientia, Varanasi, India P. 82–85.

Table 1 : Compositions of the Ayurvedic Formulations

Local Name	*Scientific Name*	*Plant Parts*	*Weight per table (mg)*
Sookshma triphala (250 mg tablet three times a day, with water after meals)			
Hirda	Terminalia Chebula	Dried Fruit	66.66
Retz	(Combrefaceae)		
Behda	Terminalia elerica	Dried Fruit	66.66
Roxb	(Combretaceae)		
Amalaki	Emblica Officinalis Gaertn Euphobiaceae	Dried Fruit	66.66
Parad	Mercury Pure	(Mineral)	5
Gandhak	Sulphur	(Mineral)	5
Thiostanin (250 mg table three times a day, with water after meals)			
Gandhak	Sulphur pure	(Mineral)	84
Vanga Bhasma	Tin Pure	(Mineral)	66
Parad	Mercury Pure	(Mineral)	5
Lohabhasma	Ferrous Sulphet	(Mineral)	3
Abhrak Bhasma	Mica	(Mineral)	4
Tamara Bhasma	Copper	(Mineral)	3
Hidra	Terminalia Chebula	Dried Fruit	3
Beheda	Terminalia balerica Roxb	Dried Fruit	2
Amlaki	Emblica Officinalis Gaertn	Dried Fruit	2
Shilajit	Asphalt	(Mineral)	7
Guggul	Commiphora Mukul (Buseraceae)	Flook ex stocks	9
Chitrak	Plumbago Zeylanica Linn	Root	9
Kutki	Picrorrhiza Kurroa Linn	Root	9
Placebo (250 mg tablet, three times a day with water after meals)			

(Contd...)

Local Name	*Scientific Name.*	*Plant Parts*	*Weight per table (mg)*
	Charcoal I.P.	Carbon	125
	Lactose	Carbon	100
	Excipients	hydrate	25
Shankhabhasma Vati (250 mg tablet three times a day, with water, after meals)			
	Counch (from sea)	(Mineral)	250
Kutaj	Holarrhena antidysenterica Linn	Stem skin (Apcoynaceal)	180
Amalaki	Emblica Officinalis Gaertn (Euphorbiaceae)	Dried Fruit	30
Vidang	Embleica ribes Burn (Myrsinaceae)	Dried Fruit	30
Sunth	Zingiber officinale Roscoe (Zingiberacae)	Rizome	10

Table 2 : Demographic characteristic of the patients on entry.

Description Group	*1*	*2*	*3*	*4*	*5*
Number of Patients	16	17	15	14	20
Male/Female	10/6	9/8	6/9	7/7	10/10
Age (yrs) Mean	21.2	20.8	22.0	21.2	20.2
range	18–25	18–26	18–25	18–26	18–25
Pulse rate (per minute)	82 ± 2.6	80 ± 6.0	81 ± 5.0	86 ± 4	82 ± 4
Body weight (Kg)	50.2	48.2	51	50.4	52.4
Flook ex stocks (Burseraceae)	± 2.8	± 6.0	2.8	± 1.6	± 6.0
Complexion					
Fair	8	10	10	7	10
Brown	8	7	5	7	10

(Contd...)

Description Group	*1*	*2*	*3*	*4*	*5*
Diet					
Vegetarian	12	15	10	10	12
Nonvegetarian	4	2	5	4	8
Smokes	2	3	2	4	5

Table 3 : Reasons for Patients Failing to Complete Trial Reason Number of Patients

Group	*1*	*2*	*3*	*4*	*5*
Lack of reasons					
Side Effect	3	2	3	1	2
Personal Reasons	1	1	2	0	1
Total	4	3	5	1	3
Patient successfully completing trial	13	14	10	13	18

Table 4 : Changes in inflammatory lesions during treatment Figures are mean + SD

Group	*Initial*	*Weeks of treatment*		
		2	*4*	*6*
1. I.	22.2 ± 4.0	26.2 ± 2.0	24.2 ± 1.8	18.0 ± 4.0
2. II.	20.3 ± 2.0	20.4 ± 3.0	18.0 ± 2.0	16.4 ± 2.4
3. III.	24.3 ± 4.0	23.2 ± 2.0	24.2 ± 1.4	20.4 ± 4.0
4. IV.	24.3 ± 3.8	22.0 ± 2.4	18.0 ± 4.0	17.4 ± 4.2
5. V.	24.3 ± 4.2	16.4 ± 2.4	12.4 ± 2.4	10.2 ± 3.6

Table 5 : Changes in inflammatory lesions during treatment

Group	*Initial*	*Weeks of treatment*		
		2	*4*	*6*
1. I.	50.2 ± 7.0	50.0 ± 6.0	48.2 ± 4.2	46.0 ± 2.0
2. II.	48.4 ± 6.2	47.0 ± 6.2	46.2 + 2.4	45.2 + 4.0
3. III.	51.2 ± 6.8	50.4 ± 4.2	46.2 ± 4.2	46.4 ± 2.8
4. IV.	49.0 ± 6.2	48.2 ± 4.2	50.2 ± 4.2	46.2 ± 2.8
5. V.	51.4 ± 6.2	44.2 ± 4.9	40.2 ± 1.4	35.2 ± 4.0

CHAPTER 11

CLINICAL ASSESSMENT OF MIXTURE OF KHADIRARISHTA, MAHAMANJISHTHADI KWATH AND SARIVADYASAVA IN THE SUBTLE FORM *i.e.*, DC 3X GLOBULES, IN VARIOUS SKIN DISORDERS

Prof. P.H. Kulkarni

Introduction

Skin disorder is very common complaint in day to day medical practice. Khadirarishta, Mahamanjishthadi kwath and Sarivadyasava are Ayurvedic herbal product, manufactured by Ayurved Rasashala, Pune (India) are useful in complaints of skin.

It was thought to prepare the said mixture of sookshma (subtle) form and clinical trials be conducted. It was further decided to conduct such clinical trials for its efficacy, safety and low cost.

Methodology

A (*i*) Mixture of khadirarishta, mahamanjishthadi kwath and Sarivadyasava mixed in equal proportion, and one par mixed in nine parts of Alcohol water mixture. Mixture was alcohol 42% and Distilled water 58% and kept for 24 hours on shelf after shaking well the mixture (Mist DC 1X).

(*ii*) One part of mist 1X and nine parts of Alcohol water mixture as mentioned above. It was stirred well kept 24 hours on shelf (Mist DC 2X).

(*iii*) One part of mist 2X and nine parts of alcohol water mixture as mentioned above. It was stirred well and kept 24 hours on shelf (mist DC 3X)

(*iv*) One ml. of Mist 3X was sprinkled on 50 gms. of sugar globules bearing no. 30 globules and mist 3x was mixed vigorously on plain porcelin oval shaped plate and kept open for few minutes. Then all globules treated with mist DC 3X globules were transferred to glass container.

B. (*i*) 4 globules of above mentioned preparation *i.e.*, DC 3X three times a day was prescribed for each patient.

(*ii*) Patients were selected at Out Patient Department on random basis without consideration of age, sex, race and occupation etc.

(*iii*) Patients were checked periodically and findings were recorded.

(*iv*) DC 3X globules were also tried on patients from Australia, Newzealand and some countries of Europe, However those patients are not included in this study.

C. (*i*) DC globules contains 37 plant extracts as ingredients in subtle (Sookshma) form.

(*ii*) Main ingredients are Sarwia, Manjishtha Khadira.

(*iii*) Rasa : (Taste)

Tikta (Bitter) –27 plants

Khshaya (Astringent) –18 plants

Katu (Pungent) –17 plants

(*iv*) Veerya (Potency) of 24 ingredients is Ushna (hot) and sheeta (cold) of 13 plants.

(*v*) Vipaka (post digestive effect) 30 in cases of Katu and 04 in cases of Madhur (sweet).

(*vi*) 24 ingredients are dry (Ruksha) in nature and 24 arae light (Laghu) in nature.

Observations

Age Group	*No. of Patients*	*%*
1 month–12 months	02	04
1 year–10 years	08	16
11 year–20 years	07	14
21 year–30 years	07	14
31 year–40 years	09	18
41 year–50 years	09	18
51 year–60 years	05	10
61 year–70 years	03	06
Total	50	100

Sex group	*No. of Patients*	*%*
1. Female	22	44
2. Male	28	56
Total	50	100

Occupation	*No. of Patients*	*%*
1. Student	15	30
2. Tailor	01	02

(Contd...)

	Occupation	*No. of Patients*	*%*
3.	Household	09	18
4.	Artist	01	02
5.	Retired	04	08
6.	Telephone Operator	01	02
7.	Contractor	01	02
8.	Doctor	01	02
9.	Service	10	20
10.	Business	03	06
11.	Nothing Particular	03	06
12.	Chartered Accountant	01	02
	Total	50	100

	Prakruti	*No. of Patients*	*%*
1.	Kapha Pitta	11	22
2.	Pitta Kapha	18	36
3.	Kapha Vata	01	02
4.	Vata Kapha	00	00
5.	Vata Pitta	08	16
6.	Pitta Vata	12	24
	Total	50	100

	Symptom Wise	*No. of Patients*
1.	Pigmentation	19
2.	Cracked Soles/Palms	02
3.	Vitiligo	02
4.	Hansen's	01
5.	Eczema	11
6.	Dry skin	06
7.	Paronichia	01
8.	Acne	04

(Contd...)

	Symptom Wise	*No. of Patients*
9.	Fungal	01
10.	Pruritus	08
11.	Varicose veins	01
12.	Haemangioma	02

No. of days treatment		*No. of Patients*	*%*
1.	30	13	26
2.	42	01	02
3.	60	06	12
4.	90	28	56
5.	180	01	02
6.	1000	01	02
	Total	50	100

	Relief	*No. of Patients*	*%*
1.	Fair–30% relief	09	18
2.	Moderate–60% relief	21	42
3.	Excellent–80% relief	20	40
	Total	50	100

Discussion

(*i*) Incidence of skin complaints observed in all age groups nearly in equal proportion.

(*ii*) Considering occupation of patients, students, service and household patients formed major bulk of patients.

(*iii*) Pittakapha, Pittavata and Kaphapitta prakruti patients found more prone to skin complaints.

(*iv*) Skin pigmentation, eczema and pruritis formed major group.

(*v*) 56% patients needed 90 days for correcting skin problem and 26% required 30 days.

(*vi*) Every patient got relief from his skin complaint. However 82% patients got more than 60% relief and that is important highlight of this study.

(*vii*) DC globules correct this skin problems by acting on levels of Agni (Enzyme), Dosha (Energy) and Dhatu (Tissue).

Conclusion

DC 3X globules are palatable, safe, economical and useful in skin diseases occurring in general medical practice.

Acknowledgement

Thanks are due to Ayurveda Rasashala for sponsoring the project and Institute of Indian Medicine for research facilities and references.

REFERENCES

1. Dr. Kulkarnin P.H. Ayurveda for you, Sagar Prakashan, Pune–29 (India), 1992.
2. Dr. Palkar and Dr. Kulkarni, Aushadhi Sangraha, Ayurveda Rasashala, Pune–4, (India), 1994.

CHAPTER 12

USE OF VRANSHODHAN TAILA IN CASE OF DARUNAKA (DANDRUFF)

Vd. Mrs. Praphullata P. Suru & (Guide) Prof. Dr. P.H. Kulkarni

Hair which have protective function in case of animal has more cosmetic value in man. The rate of growth, the texture of hair differ in various areas of body as well as in individuals too. Unhygenic conditions, no care and presence of dandruff retards growth of hair considerably. Now-a-day due to awareness of personality and self-consciousness of patients, the patients are very much interested to get rid of dandruff with help of non-toxic natural sourced Ayurvedic Medicines. So selected Dandruff–Darunaka as a subject of my research.

About Darunaka there is comparatively less information in Ayurvedic text.

दारूणा कण्डुरा रूक्षा केशभूमि : प्रपायते।
कफमारूत कोपेन विद्यानारूणांक तु तम्।।

It is mentioned in Sushrut Sanhita Sushrutacharya considered Darunaka as a क्षुद्ररोग (minor disease) which affects केशभूमी (scalp) the word mainly applicable to scalp. This disease takes place as a result of vitiation of humours कफ (Kapha) and वात (Vata) making the hair and scalp dry with lot of itching at केशभूमी वाग्भटाचार्य (scalp) considered this disease as a शिरोरोग (head disease) as this disease affects mainly scalp.

According to the Allopathic science this disease dandruff, the other name in 'Seborrhic Capitalia' is due to abnormal keratinization of the epidermal cells. That means this disease occurs due to excess formation of Keratin, which occurs mainly in young pts.

'Darunaka' though not hazardous is responsible to create lot of irritation and annoyance, because there is severe itching and very peculiar shading of scally layers thro' the skin, especially in the scalp. This disease is many times neglected and then it spreads on nearby areas like back, neck, etc. gives rise to generalised Seborrhic Dermatitis.

According to Allopathic science there is no curative treatment. It is observed that so many youngsters complain of this disease and are not getting way through it. There are so many anti–dandruff shampoos available in the market, but in some patients these shampoos create irritation of skin or eyes. Therefore a thought of harmless remedy for this type of problem came forward.

The allopathic Doctors and beauticians usually advise the patients of dandruff not to use oil, because with usual oils like coconut oil, there are chances of spread of organism pityriosporum ovale.

On Ayurvedic view, this disease is affecting mainly the skin and the vitiation of Vat is predominant so thought of external application of oil on the skin. Because the disease is peculiar with its dryness and rough feel. Now while selecting the oil it is essential that the oil should be कफवातघ्न (Anti Kapha-Vata).

Coconut oil is Madhur (Sweet) and Sheeta (Cold), so though वातशामक (antivata) it increases कफ (kapha). So the oil 'Vranashodhan Taila' was selected. It is a proprietory medicine of Ayurved Rasashala, Pune 411 004. Because it is having base of Karanja taila (करंज तेल) which is वातकफनाशक (anti Vata-Kapha), चर्मरोगहर (anti skin disease), कृमीनाशक (wormicidal) and व्रणशोधक (wound cleaner) Other contents of वर्णशोधन तेल (Vranashodhan oil) are–

1. Nimba – Azadiracta Indica
2. Nirgundi – Vitex Negundo
3. Dhattur – Datura Fastuosa
4. Karveer – Nerium Oleander
5. Haritaki – Terminalia Chebulla

Nimba is Snigdha (oily), Laghu (light), ushna (hot) krumighna (antiworm). Nirgudi is Ushna Krumikushthagna and Dhattura is Kandughna, Ushna Vranaghna Karveer is Krumi kandughna, Kushthaghna Haritaki is Vranaghna with specific property–युकालिक्षाविनाशन.

So all these properties are against Kapha, Vata and skin disorders.

For this research project patients were selected at random and irrespective of age, sex, socio economic conditions.

The way of application was as follows. All the patients were advised to apply व्रणशोधन तेल (vranashodhan oil) on the areas where dandruff was present, especially scalp twice in a week, for 5 week, that, is total 10 application. Patients were advised to apply oil at night with fingerstips on scalp and not on the hair. They were advised to do the amount of oil was not fixed, only the pt were advised to apply oil on total scalp gentle massage for 2–3 minutes and were advised pt. to keep oil over there for whole night. Next morning hair wash was advised, but washing with soap was strictly prohibited.

After 10 applications observation were made and in patients who did not had satisfactory relief further 10 applications were advised. No oral medications were given. No diet restrictions were advised.

Total 78 patients were treated amongst which no patient dropped out. This really shows awareness of patients about this problem. After finishing the course of 10 or 20 applications recheck was done first after 3 months and than after 6 months.

In patients 43 were female and 35 males.

The age group was ranging between 15 to 34 yrs.

Maximum patients were between 15 to 30 yrs.

The patient those showed total absence in dandruff after 10 applications were considered as best result–There were 57 patients of this type.

In rest 21 patients though dandruff was less it was still existing, hence further applications were advised.

In 18 pts after 20 applications the dandruff was no more.

Only in 3 patients though dandruff was less as it was present still in considerable amount they were considered as no results.

Very few patients complained of the disagreeable smell. But some patients mentioned that as compared to some antidandruff Shampoos the smell is tolerable. No major side effect was complained of.

I will like to tell one case. There was a lady of 41 yrs. She had spread of dandruff in eyebrows and ever in eyelashes. She was having considerable mental stress. She was advised to apply व्रणशोधन तेल on scalp, forehead and even eyebrows of course she was not advised to apply it on eyelashes. She had scaly patches on the junction of hair and the forehead. No oral medication was given in 10 applications all complaints disappeared and even after 6 months rechecking there was no recurrence.

In other cases after 3 months rechecking 7 patients got recurrence, who had shown best results initially, *i.e.*, in no dandruff after 10 applications only. They were advised to take further 10 applications.

After 6 months recheking 32 pts had recurrence. 24 of them were from best result obtained group and 08 were from moderate result obtained group.

So as the percentage of recurrence was considerable it can be concluded that this disease is not totally cured only with Vranashodhan Taila, but recurrence is delayed. Also there is no side effect, hence Vranashodhan tail is safe external application treatment in dandruff.

Darunaka, though not curative Vranashodhak tail is safe external application treatment in dandruff. Darunaka, though not curative Vranashodhak Tail with periodic applications may prove useful as a preventive treatment.

Acknowledgement

I will like to remains in debt of my guide Dr. P.H. Kulkarni for his valuable guidance.

I thank Ayurved Rasashala for providing me this Medicine and their help.

CHAPTER 13

SKIN DISEASES AND SOOKSMA TRIPHALA

Prof. Dr. A.A. Kaid (Germany) &
Prof. Dr. P.H. Kulkarni

Introduction

Skin problems/disorders are very common all over the world. Claim about **Sookshma Triphana** was that it is useful in majority of skin problems, as well as without any side effects and economical also. Hence we decided to conduct clinical trials of Sookshma Triphala in various skin complaints.

About Sookshma Triphala

It is proprietory Ayurvedic Medicine of Ayurvedic Rasashala, Pune (India).

Contents : Each Tablet of 250 mgs. contains

1.	Hareetaki	Terminalia Chebula	66.7 mg.
2.	Bibheetaka	Terminalia Bellerica	66.7 mg.
3.	Amalaki	Emblica Officinalis	66.7 mg.
4.	Kajjali made from :		
(*i*)	Shuddha Parada	Detoxified Mercury	5.0 mg.
(*ii*)	Shuddha Gandhaka	Detoxified Sulphar	5.0 mg.

Triphala the basic constituent of this drug is useful in Kapha and Pitta disorders. Kajjali enhances the action of Triphala and reaches to minute tubules, cells etc.

This compound is useful in skin disease and as a blood purifier. It is used as a primary antibiotic and can safely be prescribed during or after withdrawal of broad spectrum antibiotics for prevention of re–infections.

With warm astringent action it alleviates "Kapha Dosha". Thus relieves inflammatory conditions by preventing pus formation.

It is successfully used in viral infections, long lasting fevers and as a drug of choice in Acne vulgaries.

Ayurvedic View and Management of Kushtha (Skin Disease)

Definition : The disease which disturbs skin structure and functions of skin (Sharir sapta dhatu) is known as 'KUSHTHA' (Skin Diseases).

Srotasa (affected) : Raktavaha Srotasa

Types : 18 types

(*a*) 7 Maha Kushtha Kapala, Audumbara, Mandal, Rusnajivna Dadru, Kakanak Pundarik.

(*b*) 11 Kshudra kushtha Ek Kushtha Charma Kushtha Kitibha, Vipadika Alasaka, Shataru, Pama Visphota, Vicharchika.

Causes

(*i*) Viruddhashana (Incompatibale food intake).

(*ii*) Adhyashana (Over eating).

(*iii*) Navanna Sevan (Fresh grain food intake).

(*iv*) Dahi (Curds) + Matsya (fish), Mulak (radish), Masha (Black gram), Til (Sesame), Gud (jaggery) Sevan (Consumption).

(*v*) Lavan–Amla Sevana (Sour and Salty food intake).

(*vi*) Mutra Vega dharana (Avoided urination), Mala (Defaecation), Vamana (Emesis), Vegdharan. (*i.e.*, Avoiding (1) Urination, (2) Defeacation, (3) Emesis).

(*vii*) Ati Vyayam (Excessive exercise).

(*viii*) Diva swapna (Day Time Sleeping).

(*ix*) Papa karma (ill–deeds).

Purvaroop (pre-symptoms)

(*i*) Twak Shlakshnata, Ruksha (Skin becomes soft or dry).

(*ii*) Vrana Shighrotpatti Chirasthiti (wound appears very quickly but healing delayed).

(*iii*) Daha (burning sensation).

(*iv*) Toda (pricking sensation).

(*v*) Kandu (itching sensation).

(*vi*) Klama (exhaustion).

(*vii*) Atisweda or Asveda Pravritti (excessive sweating/ no sweet).

(*viii*) Romaharsha (Light Shivering).

Roopa (Signs and Symptoms)

(*i*) Rookshata (Dryness of skin).

(*ii*) Shosha (Loosing Flesh).

(*iii*) Toda (Pricking).

(*iv*) Shoola (Pain).

(*v*) Sankocha (Constriction).

(*vi*) Shyava/Arun Varna (Blackish/reddish colour).

(*vii*) Daha (Burning).

(*viii*) Lalima (Redness).

(*ix*) Srava–Serous discharge.

(*x*) Anga Patan (Loss of elasticity of skin).

(*xi*) Kandu (Pruritus).

(*xii*) Krumiyukta (Contaminated).

Samprapti (pathogenesis)

- Dosha Prakop (Dosha).
- Tiryak Sira Pravesha (Abnormal circulation).
- Twak Mansa, Rakta, Lasika Dushti (Vitiation of skin, muscle, blood and lymph).
- Dhatu Shaithilya (Loose Dhatu).
- Twak Vaivarnya (Changed colour of skin).
- Kushtha (Skin Diseases).

Chikitsa

A. Shodhana (Purification) (Cleansing)

(*i*) Ghritapaan (Ghee intake)–Dashamul, Guduchi, Eranda, Ghrita.

(*ii*) Vaman (Emesis)–After every 15 days.

(*iii*) Virechan (Purgation)–Once in a month Nishottar, Danti, Triphala.

(*iv*) Rakta Mokshan (Blood letting) Jalouka, Shringa, Alabu, Siravedha. Done every 6 months.

(*v*) Shirovirechan–Vidanga Churna, Marich Churna.

(*vi*) Basti (Enema) (*a*) Nirooha (Oil + decoction), (*b*) Anuvasana. (Oil).

B. Shamana (Paliative)

(*i*) Abyanga–For external application = Lepa–Mansyado Lepa Kushthadi Lepa, Karanjabeeja Lepa.

(*ii*) Snehapan (oleation)–Tiktaka Ghrita.

(*iii*) Shatadhauta Ghrita, Vajrak Ghrita, Vajrak Taila.

(*iv*) Ekeri (Single)–Khadir, Nimba, Chandan (Sandle wood) Manjishtha.

(*v*) Churna (Powder)–Mashadi, Triphaladi Churna.

(*vi*) Anupan–Ghee + Honey.

(*vii*) Ghrita–Tiktaka Ghrita, Mahatiktaka Ghrita.

(*viii*) Taila (Oil)–Kushthadya, Kanakakshiri.

(*ix*) Asava (Medicated wines) Madhvasav, Triphalasava Sarivadyasava.

(*x*) Arishta (Medicated wine) Khadirarishta – 20–40 ml and 20–4 ml water.

(*xi*) Leha (Jam)–Amla, Mandur, Pippali, Vidanga, Leha 500 mgm 3 times a day.

Daivyapashraya Chikitsa

(*i*) Vrata, Indriya Nigraha (Control over the body senses).

(*ii*) Mano Nigraha (Control over the mind).

(*iii*) Guru, Mata, Pita Seva (Service to Teacher mother and father).

Pathya (*Do*) : Sadharan Aahar (normal diet), Mano Nigraha (Mind control).

Apathya (*Don't*) : Lavan (Avoid salt), Amla (Sour), Ushna (hot) Katu Aahar (Pungent food).

Methodology

(*i*) Patients were selected on random basis at Out Patient Department, irrespective of age, sex and occupation.

(*ii*) Every patient received 2 tablets three times a day with water.

(*iii*) Patients were reviewed every two weeks and recorded the progress.

(*iv*) Patients were also treated in following countries Germany. Czechoslovakia, Australia, New Zealand. However those cases are not included in this study.

Observations

Age Group : Analysis of observation is as follows :

Sr. No.	*From–To years*	*No. of Patient*
1.	0–10	08
2.	11–20	18
3.	21–30	15
4.	31–40	10
5.	41–50	10
6.	51–60	02
7.	61–70	02
	Total	65

Sexwise

1.	Female	43
2.	Male	22
	Total	65

Prakrutiwise

Sr. No.	*Type*	*No. of Patients*
1.	Vatapitta	25
2.	Pitta Vata	15
3.	Pitta Kapha	16
4.	Kaphapitta	09
5.	Kaphavata	–
6.	Vatakapha	–
	Total	65

Skin Disorders

Sr. No.	*Type of Disorders*	*No. of Patients*
1.	Eczema	12
2.	Acne	22
3.	Pruritus	15
4.	Contact detmatitis	34
5.	Dark pigmentation	03
6.	Inflammation/cellulitis	02
7.	Pityriasis Versicolor	02
8.	Paronychia	01
9.	Boils	18
10.	Dandruff	

Relief

1.	Moderate 30%	00
2.	Good 60%	15
3.	Excellent 80%	50
	Total	65

Days of Treatment

Sr. No.	*No. of Days*	*No. of Patients*
1.	07	04
2.	14	07
3.	21	29
4.	42	19
5.	84	06
		65

Discussion

Triphala is mentioned in the treatment of skin disorders in classical work of Ayurveda for virechana *i.e.,* Shodhan (purification) treatment as well as shaman treatment. Sookshma Triphala contains Triphala as well as Kajjali. Kajjali serves purpose of shodhan Shamana and above all it is yogavahi *i.e.,* enters into tiny channels *i.e.,* upto cell level in the Human body.

It seems that Vata/pitta Dosha predominant prakruti is more prone to skin diseases, Triphala is Tridoshanashaka means corrects disturbed functions of three doshas.

Some patients having more than two complaints and duration of illness was variable.

80% patients got relief in the category of excellent *i.e.,* more than 80% symptoms were relieved.

Duration of treatment was from one week to six weeks. Patients in the category of Good result may show excellent result if treatment would have been continued for another equal span of time. Of course those observations are not incorporated in this paper.

Triphala and Kajjali are described as Rasayana also in the Ayurvedic Texts. Hence it helped recovered faster and better.

Sookshma Triphala found as antibacterial as well as antiviral in some other studies.

It is needed to have further multidisceptionary studies for exact mode of action of Sookshma Triphala at various Dhatu level as well as Rasayan effect.

Conclusion

Sookshma Triphala Tablets are useful in various skin disorders without any side effects and it is very economical.

Acknowledgements

Thanks are due to Ayurvedic Rasashala, Pune for sponsoring the project and Institute of Indian Medicine for research facilities and references.

REFERENCES

1. Abhang Ranjana : Triphala in the modern investigation. Deerghayu International, Vol II, 4 June 1986.
2. Bopegamage Shubhada, A Petrovicova : The antiviral effect of the Ayurvedic preparation–sookshma. Triphala on different cosaxckie viruses and Rotavirus sa II and the influence of this preparation on GMK and MA–104 Cell lines, Ayurveda Research papers. Ayurveda Rasashala, Pune–411004
3. Channa : Basappa : Action of Triphala, H.P.A., P.G.T.C.A. (I.S.A.R.) Jamnagar, 1965.
4. Kulkarni P.H. : Ayurveda for you, Sagar Prakashan, Pune–411029, 1992.
5. Kulkarni Sunita and Karambelkar M.B. : L Mukhadoshika (Ace Vulgaris) and Sookshma Triphala, Fellow Theses, Institute of Indian. Medicine Pune, 1968.
6. Palkar and Kulkarni : Aushadhi Sangraha, and Ayurveda Rasashala, Pune–4, 1994.
7. Paranjape Prakash and Kulkarni P.H. : Comparative Efficacy of four Ayurvedic formulations in the treatment of Acne Vulgaris : A double blind randomised placebo controlled clinical evaluation– Ayurvedic research papers, ayurveda Rasashala, Pune–1, 1994.

CHAPTER 14

CLINICAL EVALUATION OF 'MAHAMANJISHTHADI QUATH AND SOOKSHMA TRIPHALA' IN THE MANAGEMENT OF ACNE VULGARIS

Dr. Prakash Paranjpe

Summary

Forty patients with Acne Vulgaris were randomised into four groups. Three different Ayurvedic treatment schedules were given orally for 8 weeks; while one group received placebo. Physical and clinical investigations were carried out at every two weeks intervals. A significant reduction in lesion count was observed in patients receiving combination of two drugs (Group A) when compared with placebo and other two Ayurvedic formulations which failed to produce any significant difference from the pre–treatment condition. The drugs were well tolerated.

Key Words

Ayurvedic formulations; Acne Vulgaris; Clinical trial.

Introduction

Acne Vulgris, a chronic inflammatory disorder of the pilosebaceous follicles, is an important disorder for which medical treatment is commonly sought in the clinical practice. It is a major cause for both psychological and social disability and the rate of unemployment amongst young adults with acne is significantly higher in both males and females (Motley and Finaly 1989, Cunliffe 1986). Treating Acne has become a problems since sate drugs are not used for a long time though they are not completely free from adverse effects. The use of clindamycin may cause pseudomembranous colitis (Milestone *et. al.*, 1981), tetracycline may colour the skin yellow and erythromycin may precipitate hepatic dysfunction (Coskay 1975). Though effective isotretinion causes untowards effects with greater frequency including risk teratogenicity (Lammer 1985). There is a clear need for a safer and effective drug for long term therapy of Acne Vulgaris.

Ayurvea is the ancient science of life. In the Sanskrit language, "Ayu" means life and "Veda" means knowledge. The branch of medicine has a very old record of use in the Indian system of medicine (Paranjpe *et. al.,* 1990). Charak Samhita, an Ayurvedic classic describes acne Vene Vulgaris as "Tarunya Peetika" meaning a disease of adolescence. A variety of drugs have been used in the Ayurvedic system of medicine to treat this condition. These agents are Sookshma. Thiphala. Mahamanjishthadi Quath etc., and are claimed to be safe and effective (Sharangdhar Samhita 1984) but their effectiveness have not been tested in controlled clinical trials. Hence we took randomised, singleblind placebo controlled clinical trial of these agents in the treatment of Acne vulgaris.

Materials and Methods

Ayurvedic Medicines

The composition of the three formulations is detailed in table 1, and were obtained from Ayurveda Rasashala, Pune.

Clinical Studies

Twenty two male and eighteen female patients between the age of 18 and 28 with facial acne were recruited at Nanal hospital Pune patient were recruited on the basis of having moderate acne vulgaris of the face manifested by at least 10 popular of pustules and at least 5 open or closed comedones. Patients with known hypersensitivity to drugs and those contemplating pregnancy were not admitted into the trial. At the time of entry into the study, they were biochemically nondiabetic. The non diabetic state was confirmed by estimation of fasting blood sugar levels (100 mg%). All topical and systemic acne treatment and medications, if any, were discontinued at least two weeks before entry into the study. Demographic characters of patients on entry are recorded in Table 2. During the study period patients were requested not to take any other medicaments and no instructions were given to the patients concerning the diet and the mechanical removal of comedones. Written informed consent and detailed clinical history was obtained from the patients. They were randomised into four groups and the patients group did not differ significantly with regard to sex, age, diet, smoking status etc.

Dosage and Care Regimen

Medication was taken orally, three tablets twice daily and/or 25 ml of decoction of Mahamanjishtha in the afternoon and at bed time after food. Patients were advised to wash their face with a mild soap regularly.

Clinical Evaluation

The clinical evaluation was done, every two weeks, by counting the inflammatory and noninflammatory lesions on the face. For the purpose of analysis, papules and pustules were combined as inflammatory lesions and open and closed comedones were combined as noninflammatory lesions (Allen and Smith, 1982). The patient's compliance was assessed by counting tablets and the decoction in the tablet container or the bottle. Facial photographs (transparencies) were taken initially and at the end of the study.

Data Analysis

Stastical analysis of lesions count was performed on raw scores employing and analysis of variance (ANOVA) for repeated measures to assess change in each patient group over eight weeks treatment period. Demographic data and overall response data were analysed by nonparametric Chi Square analysis.

Results

Thirty four patients completed the study and there were six dropouts during the course of it study. The patients dropouts were due to various reasons including not getting benefit, domestic reasons and family problems (Table 3). The findings for the changes in the total number of inflammatory lesions are summarised in Table 4. The drug group did not differ significantly before treatment for the lesions in this category Treatment with combination of Sookshma Triphala and Mahamanjishthadi Quath (Group A) was associated with significant reduction (PS 0.001) in lesion count by the end of the treatment period. The findings for change in the total number of non–inflammatory lesions are given in Table 5. Initial lesions count were comparable in all the treatment groups. Treatment with combination (Group A) was associated with significant reduction in this lesion category. As far as overall change in facial acne condition is concerned, the treatment in group A showed excellent response. The drug therapy in all the groups was well tolerated.

Discussion

In the present study, two Ayurvedic formulations, separately and in combination and placebo were given in randomly allocated groups of acne vulgaris patients. Treatment in Group A showed a significant improvement in the severity of both, inflammatory and non-inflammatory lesions. However treatment in groups failed to show any significant improvement in the severity of both, inflammatory and non-inflammatory lesions. However treatment in groups failed to show any significant improvement in the severity of acne. The response to treatment in Group A is comparable to the results reported from other well controlled trials using antibiotics and other agents (Dobson and Belknap 1980, Malski and Arndt 1980). The exact mechanism of action of this novel Ayurvedic combination (Group A) has not yet been worked out. Whether this drug has any antiseptic and or anti–inflammatory activity remains to be investigated. Further work is essential to investigate the long term effects and efficiency of this combination.

Conclusion

Among the three Ayurvedic formulations tried in the present clinical trial, only combination of Mahamanjishthadi Quath and Sookshma Triphala was found to be orally effective in the treatment of Acne Vulgaris. These all drugs were well tolerated.

Acknowledgement

We thank Dr. P.H. Kulkarni, president, Ayurveda Rasashala, Pune, for sponsoring the clinical trial. The management of Nanal Hospital, Pune, deserves thanks for providing the facilities. Special thanks to Dr. P.S. Patki for design of protocol.

REFERENCES

1. Charak Samhita (1949). Translated by Shree Gulabkunverba Ayurvedic Society, Jamnagar, India. p. 58.
2. Coskey R.J. (1975) Side effects of antibiotics therapy in acne vulgaris, Cutis 15, 710–712.
3. Cunliffe W.J. (1986). Acne and unemployment. British Journal of Dermatology 115, 386–388.
4. Dobson R.L. and Belknap B.S. (1980). Topical erythromysin solution in acne, Journal of American Academy of Dermatology 3, 478–482.
5. Lammer E.J. (1985). Retinoic acid embryopathy. New England Journal of Medicine 313, 837–841.
6. Mals J.M. and Amdt K.A. (1980). Topical therapy for acne. New Zealand Journal of Medicine, 302, 503–506.
7. Milstone E.B. Mc Donald A.J. Socholhamer C.F. (1981). Pseudomembranous colitis after topical application of clindamycin. Archieves of Dermatology 117, 154–155.
8. Motley R.J. and Finlay A.Y. (1990). Practical use of disability index in the routine management of double blind placebo controlled clinical trial. Journal of Ethnopharmacology 29, 1–11.
9. Paranjpe P., Patki P., Patwardhan B. (1990). Ayurvedic treatment of obesity : A randomised double blind placebo controlled clinical trial. Journal of Ethnopharmacology 29, 1–11.
10. Sharangdhar Samhita (1984). Translated by Shrikanta Murti, Chaukhambha Orientia, Varanasi India, P. 82–85.

Table 1 : Compositions of the Ayurvedic Formulations

Local Name	*Scientific*	*Weight*
1. Sookshma Triphala 250 mg tablet		
Hirda	Terminalia chebula	66.66 mg
Beheda	Teminalia belerica	66.66 mg

(Contd...)

Local Name	*Scientific*	*Weight*
Amalaki	Emblica Officinalis	66.66 mg
Parad	Mercury Pure	5.00 mg
Gandhak	Sulphar Pure	5.00 mg
2. Placebo 250 mg Tablet		
Amalaki Mashi	Emblica officinalis (ash)	150 mg
Takan lahi	Borax Pure	33 mg
Sajjikshar	Salt	33 mg
Hing	Asaffoetida	16 mg
3. Mahamanjishthadi Quath (Syrup–Each 10 ml Contains)		
Manjishtha	Rubia cordiflia	100 mg
Kadunimb Saal	Melia azadirachta	100 mg
Adulsa	Adhatoda vasica	100 mg
Triphala	Hirda–Beheda–Amalaki	100 mg
Chitrak	Plumbago zeylanica	100 mg
Halad	Curcuma longa	100 mg
Daruhalad	Berberis aristata	100 mg
Gulvel	Tinospora cordifolia	100 mg
Kadechirait	Swertia chirayita	100 mg
Khair Saal	Acacia catechu	100 mg
Kutki	Picronhiza	100 mg
Bavchi	Psoralia corylifolia	100 mg
Amalavetas	Garcinia pedunculata	100 mg
Morwel	Marsedenia tenacissima	100 mg
Dantimool	Baliospermum montanum	100 mg
Indrayan	Citrullus colocynthis	100 mg
Vavding	Embelia ribes	100 mg
Jatamansi	Nordostachys jafamansi	100 mg
Trayman	Gentiana kurroa	100 mg
Pahadmool	Cocculus hirsutus	100 mg
Nishottar	Operculina turpethum	100 mg
Anantmool	Hemidesmul indicus	100 mg
Kadu Padwal	Trichosanthes dioica	100 mg
Mire	Piper nigrum	100 mg
Pimpli	Piper longum	100 mg

Table 2 : Demographic Characteristic of Patients on Entry

Description	*Group A*	*Group B*	*Group C*	*Group D*
Number of patients	10	10	10	10
Male/Female 5/5	5/5	5/5	7/3	8/2
Age (yrs.) Mean	20.3	21.1	21.8	20.7
Pulse rate (per minute)	74 +–2.6	78 +–1.2	75 +–2.2	79 +–1.2
P. Syst/Diast mm Hg	116 +–5.2	118 +–2.2	119 +–5.6	110 +–4.1
Mean +–SD	82 +–1.2	78 +–2.4	76 +–4.5	78 +–1.2
Body Weight (Kg)	57.2 +–5.1	55.8 +–4.9	49.7 +–2.2	52.8 +--3.4
Diet Veg/Nonveg	8/2	7/3	6/4	9/1
Smokers	1	3	2	1
Drugs Therapy	Sookshma Triphala + Mahaman Jishthadi Quath	Mahaman Jisthadi Quath	Sookshma Triphala	Placebo (Charcosal)

Table 3 : Reason for Patients Failing to complete trial

Reasons	*Number of Patients in*			
	Group A	*Group B*	*Group C*	*Group D*
Lack of Reasons	–	1	1	2
Side effects	–	–	–	–
Personal reasons	–	1	0	1
Total	0	2	1	3
Patients successfully completing trial	10	08	09	07

Table 4 : Changes in Inflammatory Lesions during Treatment Figures are mean + –SD

Group	*Initial*	*Weeks of Treatment*			
		2	*4*	*6*	*8*
A	22	18	16	10*	7*
B	20	18	16	15	10
C	18	16	15	14	10
D	19	16	15	15	9

* P (Less than) 0.01.

Table 5 : Changes in Non-inflammatory lesions during Treatment Figures are mean +–SD

Group	*Initial*	*Weeks of Treatment*			
		2	*4*	*6*	*8*
A	68	44	34	28*	24*
B	66	60	54	50	38
C	65	58	50	46	36
D	64	60	54	46	32

* P (Less than) 0.01.

CHAPTER 15

MAHAMANJISHTHADI QUATH IN ACNE VULGARIS—A CLINICAL STUDY

Prof. Dr. K. V. Shah

Summary

Acne Vulagris Chronic inflammatory disorder of the pilosebaceous follicles and its commonly met in the general practice. Treating acne has become a problem as 'it needs prolonged treatment and numerous formulations said to be effective in Acne Vulgaris, but is in want of clinical studies. Mahamanjishthadi Quath is one of those. Hence we took a clinical trial on 30 patients of Acne Vulgaris at Nanal Hospital. The patient were classified in two groups, one receiving Mahamanjishthadi Quath and second the placebo (Amalaki mashi vati). The duration of the clinical study was six weeks.

Introduction

Acne Vulgaris, the commonly sought problem in clinical practice still remains unsolved irrespective of introduction of antibiotics, the supposed effective regimens. As there is frequency of recurrence of acne lesions, a prolonged treatment is the basic pre–requisite. For the drug should be effective, but safe too. The clinical studies show that the antibiotics like tetracycline, clindamycin, Erythrocin and Isotretinoin exert untowards side effects. So there is a clear need for a safer drug for long term therapy of acne vulgaris.

Ayurveda is the ancient science of life. The scholar Sushruta has mentioned distinctively the seven layers of skin Awabhasini, Lohita, Shweta, Tamra, Vedini, Rohini and Mamsadhara, respectively. (Sushruta Samhita 1985). Ayurveda has claimed the Acne Vulgaris (Tarunya Peetika) to be due to derangement of third and fourth *i.e.,* Shweeta and Tamra layers of the skin due to vitiation of Vata and Kapha Doshas and Rakta and Meda Dhatus.

A number of drugs have been used since centuries in the Ayurvedic system of Medicine to treat this condition. These agents are Sookshma Triphala, Shankha Bhasma, Chandraprabhavati, Arogyavardhini etc. (Sharangdhara Samhita 1984). Mahamanjishthadi Quath is one of these agents, but still not clinically verified. Therefore, we undertook a randomised clinical trial of this drug in the treatment of acne vulgaris.

Materials and Methods

Compositions of the two formulations used in the clinical trial are detailed in Table No. 1 and were obtained from the well established company Ayurveda Rasashala, Pune.

Clinical Studies

Thirty patients between the age 18 and 28 years with moderate acne were recruited in Nanal Hospital. All topical and systemic treatment and medications for acne if any, were discontinued two weeks before entry into the study. Written informed concept and detailed clinical history was obtained from the patients. They were randomised into two equal groups, one received Mahamanjishthadi Quath and the other Amalaki mashi vati.

Dosage and Care Regime

These patients were asked to wash their faces three times daily with mild soap. Medications were taken orally 2 teaspoons (*i.e.*, 10 ml) three times daily of Mahamanjishthadi Quath and two tablets of Amalakimashi Vati three times daily in respective groups. The treatment was continued for six weeks.

Clinical Evaluation

The patients were assessed clinically every two weeks *i.e.*, on the entry, on 14th day, on 28th day and at the end on 42nd day. Initially every fortnightly inflammatory and non inflammatory lesions on the face were counted until the end of the study. Patient's compliance was assessed by counting the tablets remaining in the container and the syrup in the bottle; returned by them every two weeks.

Results

Twenty three patients completed the study and there were seven dropouts during the course of the study. Two groups were given two different combinations. Group one received Mahamanjishthadi Quath in a dose 2 tsf tds, while Group two received Aamalakimashi Vati 2 Tabs tds. The group one, which received Mahamanjishthadi Quath showed 45% reduction in the lesions whereas group two, which received placebo, Amalakimashi Vati showed only 10% reduction in the lesions.

Discussion

In the present study, Ayurvedic drugs were given to unselected patients of acne randomly. Group one showed reasonable improvement in acne lesions whereas group two failed to show any reasonable improvement, which received placebo. It appears that treatment with Mahamanjishthadi Quath reduces the severity of acne produces a reasonable clinical improvement. The exact mechanism of action of this drug cannot be documented from our study. Whether this drug have any antiseptic and/or anti–inflammatory action remains to be investigated. Further work taking into considerations of Prakriti, Type of Acne (*viz*., Vataj, Pittaj, Kaphaj, etc.), severity of acne is needed to investigate the long term effect of Mahamanjishthadi Quath. During and after the six weeks drug therapy none of the patients showed any side effect.

Acknowledgement

Thanks are due to Ayurveda Rasashala, Pune for sponsoring the project, Cooperation from the management of Nanal Hospital and Institute of Indian Medicine for research facilities and references.

REFERENCES

1. Marathi Sushruta Samhita (1985) Editor Dr. P.H. Kulkarni, Sagar Prakashan, Pune Part 2, Page 111–112.
2. Sharangdhar Samhita (1984) Translated by K.K. Shrikant Murti, Chaukhamba Orienta, Varanasi, India, Page 82–85.
3. Nadkarni K.M. (1976). Indian Materia Medica, Popular Prakashan, Page 636.

Table 1 : Compositions of the Ayurvedic Formulations

Name	*Ingredients*	*Weight (per 10 ml) mg.*
MAHAMANJISHTHADI	Manjishtha	
QUATH	Adulsa	
Kadunimb Saal	Chitrak	
Triphala	Daruhalad	
Halad	Kadechirait	
Gulvel	Khair Saal	100 mg each
Raktachandan	Bavachi	
Kutki	Morwel	
Amlavetas	Indrayan	
Dantimool	Jatmansi	
Vavding	Pahadmoola	
Traymana	Anant moola	
Nishottar	Mire	
Karu Padwal	Pippali	
PLACEBO		
250 mg Tablet	Aamalki	250mg mashi

Table 2

	Drug	*Dose*	*Duration*	*Total Patients*	*Dropouts*
Group 1	Mahaman-jishthadi Quath	10 ml 3 times daily	6 weeks	15	3
Group 2	Placebo	2 Tabs 3 times daily	6 Weeks	15	4

CHAPTER 16

SARVATOBHADRA RASA IN SKIN DISEASES

Dr. V.V. Bhagwat

Introduction

Sarvatobhadra Rasa is useful in Liver Diseases, piles, spleen diseases. All types of fevers, swelling, Anaemia, worms, jaundice, bronchitis, cough, diabetes, ascites and all diseases.

There are four different 'Pathas' (formulations) named Sarvatobhadra Rasa available in Rasa–granthas. With its reference it is useful in all diseases and chosen skin disease for the experiment.

Experiment

The reference selected taken from Rasendra–sarsangraha and Rasa–ratna–samucchaya. It is also stated in Bharat bhaishajya ratnakar on page No. 323/8171.

Contents

Shuddha Mercury 1 Shuddha Sulphur 1 Tamra Bhasma 1 Abhrak Bhasma 1 Kant Loha Bhasma 1 Kajjali was made by mercury and sulphar and then all the above bhasmas were added into it with the bhavana of 'Ginger juice'. Then the tablets weighing 1 gunj (125 mg) was made.

This drug cures Liver–spleen diseases, piles. All types of Fevers, Anaemia, swelling, jaundice, worms, bronchitis, cough diabetes (Prameha). Ascitis formed by all Doshas. The drug made by 'Surmani' cures all the diseases.

Slight change was done while preparing the medicine. 'Gulvel' was decided to use as 'Anupan'. Gulvel Ghanasar (Liq. extract) was added for simplicity in the same proportion of the medicine. Ingredients were taken as follows :

Mercury	50 gm
Sulphar	50 gm
Tamra Bhasma	50 gm
Abhrak Bhasma	50 gm
Kant Loha Bhasma	50 gm

The Kajjali was made with Shuddha mercury and Shudda sulphur. Then Tamra Bhasma, Abhrak Bhasma and Loha bhasma were added. Ginger juice was added in same quantity. (250 gm) and Triturated the mixture. When the mixture was about to dry then 'Gulvel Ghanasar' was added 250 gms in wt. and triturated till the whole mixture become dry. Tablets were made weighing 250 mg each.

Clinical Trials and Observations

Sarvatobhadra Rasa was used in Sheeta pitta (Urticaria) Isab (Eczema) and Padadari (Cracked feet) 25 patients were tried for an experiment. Four patients were dropped put giving no reasons. So 21 patients were classified as follows :

Urticaria	11
Eczema	05
Cracked Feet	05

Sex–wise Classification

Male	18
Female	3

Age–wise Classification

Age Group (Yrs.)	*No.*
0–10	1
10–20	5
20–30	11
30–40	04
Total	21

Classification According to Response to Drug

Disease	*No. of Patients*	*Cured*	*Benefitted*	*Not Cured*
Urticaria	11	7	2	2
Isab	5	3	–	2
Cracking of Feet	5	3	1	1

Patients suffering from urticaria had come after having medication like steroids, antihistamines etc. From different skin specialists patients again suffer from urticaria after withdrawal of those medicines. Similarly patients suffering from Isab had already taken medication from other doctors. Being disappointed by other doctors, patients having 'Padadari' (Cracking of Feet) came for an ayurvedic medication. They had already taken drugs like antihistamines, steroids etc.

Diet Restrictions : Consumption of alcohol, Nicotine, much sour to taste food, fried food was strictly prohibited.

Dose : Patients below 10 years 250 mg TDS. Patients above 10 years 250 mg TDS. All other patients were told to take 2 tablets BD.

Anupan (Vehicle) : Water.

Duration of Treatment : 45 days. 4 patients out of 25 patients were asked to take 'Abhayadi Churna' 2 gms at the bed time as they were suffering from constipation.

Skin returned to its normal pattern with no itching sensation at all was considered as 100% cure. While improvement in the skin, pattern and less itching sensation was considered as 50% cure.

Discussion

Arogyavardhini is widely used by all vaidyas in skin diseases. It contains mercury, sulphar, Tamra Bhasma, Aabhrak Bhasma, and Loha Bhasma, Shilajit and other herbal medicines. The proportion of mercury sulphar, copper, Loha and Abhrak is much less in Arogyavardhini. While in Sarvatobhadra Rasa, mercury, sulphur, Abhrak, Loha, Tamra are in more proportion. Each 250 mg tablet contains 25 mg of each. Considering the more proportion of bhasmas in Sarvatobhadra, it is supposed to use in minimal doses.

Proportion of mercury, sulphar, Tamra, Loha and Abhrak in 250 mg. Tablet of Arogyavardhini.

Mercury	6.8 mg
Sulphar	6.8 mg
Copper (Tamra)	6.8 mg
Loha	6.8 mg
Abhrak	6.8 mg

Proportion of above elements in 250 mg.

Sarvatobhadra Rasa :

Mercury	25 mg
Sulphar	25 mg
Tamra	25 mg
Loha	25 mg
Abhrak	25 mg

Characteristics of Contents in Sarvatobhadra Rasa

1. Kajjali of mercury and sulphar was used in this medicine. The following shloka was stated on page 179 in 'Rasa–Dhatu–Prakash' by Vd. P.D. Mulay. It is taken from 'Ayurved Prakash'. Kajjali cures all the diseases if taken with proper 'Sahapana' and 'Anupana' It is good Aphrodi siac and corrects all the three doshas.
2. Tamra Bhasma was described on page 299 of Rasa Dhatu Prakash. The following shlokas were taken from Rasa Ratna Samucchaya. Parinamshoola (Duodenal ulcer) abdominal colic, anaemia, pyrexia, Gulma, Liver and spleen diseases, Agnimandya Meha (Diabetics), Piles, Sangrahani (ulcerative colitis), cough, bronchitis, Acidity, Apasmar, vomiting in Visuchika (Cholera); Conclusive disorders, Vataroga, In testical diseases, skin diseases, originated from Kapha and pitta, obesity, Garavisha, Aamvata (Rheumatrid Arthritis) were well benefitted by Tamra Bhasma with proper Anupana.
3. Characteristics of Loha Bhasma were described in Rasa–Dhatu–Prakash page 313 as follows : Kant Loha Bhasma improves instre of skin destroying annemia, Garvisha; it destroys Kshaya Roga; All

kushtas (skin diseases) improves power, Vayasthapak (lowers rate of aging), Stambhak Rasayan' and similar to Amrit it destroys all the diseases.

4. Abhrak Bhasma was stated in Rasa Dhatu Prakash Page 396. Abhrak Bhasma being Tridoshnashaka, destroys Vrana Meha (Diabetic wound), Kushtha (Skin diseases), Spleen diseases, ascites, poison and krimi (worms).

Gulwel was described in Bhavaprakash Follows (Dravyagunashastra by Kudatarkar Shastri page 445) Gulwel has Rasa Katu Tikta, Kshaya (hot) (bitter) (Ashtringent).

Veerya–Ushma.

Veepak–Madhur (Sweet).

It improves appetite (Agni) and being Deepana it is Tridoshanashak and Rasayan Thirst, burning sensation, Diabetes, Anaemia, jaundice, skin diseases, worms, pyrexia and vomiting are well benefitted by it. Kajjali is Sarvaroganashaka and Tamra Bhasma, Abhrak Bhasma and Loha Bhasma are Kushthanashak. Hence the mixture became Kushthanashaka.

Describing skin diseases in Doshadi Vidnyaneeya Adhyaya from Athsanghridaya Surtrasthana, Vagbhat stated the causitive factors.

Because of 'Raktadhikya' different diseases may from such as Visarpa (Herpes), Spleen Abscesses, Kushtha, Vata–rakta (Gout) Raktapitta, Gulma, Upakusha (Gum Diseases), jaundice, Vanga (Facial skin disease), unconsciousness, skin, eyes and urine may become reddish in colour etc.

Raktadosha is present in skin diseases and in Vimansthana charak stated that spleen and liver are the origin of Raktavaha shrotasa Impure blood is one of the causes of skin diseases and spleen and liver are origins of 'Rakta Vaha Srotasa'. Therefore, skin diseases can be treated by giving treatment on these basic organs. Sarvatobhadra Rasa is useful in liver and spleen diseases. Hence this is also useful in skin diseases.

This drug cures all the diseases only when it is given with proper Anupana. Addition of Gulvel in the basic Patha and Gulvel itself is kushthanashak. This drug has become excellent remedy for skin diseases.

Conclusion

Sarvatobhadra Rasa with Gulvel Ghanasara helps in cure of skin diseases.

Acknowledgement

My wife Sou. Neela Bhagwat helped me a lot for doing the experiment of use of Sarvatobhadra Rasa in skin diseases. She had taken an active participation in preparing the medicine. I am grateful to Dr. P.H. Kulkarni for his valuable guidance. I am also thankful to Institute of Indian Medicine for allowing me the use of place and library. Financial help was given by Ayurved Rasashala.

REFERENCES

1. Charak Samhita.
2. Sushrut Samhita.
3. Ashtanghridaya Vagbhat.
4. Madhav Nidan.
5. Rasa Dhatu Prakash–P.D. Mulay.
6. Bharat–Bhaishajya Ratnakar.
7. Ayurved Prakash.
8. Rasa Ratnakar.

Rasa Veerya Veepak of Contents

Dravya	*Rasa*	*Veerya*	*Veepak*	*Doshghnata*	*Guna*	*Ragaghanata*
Murcury	All six	Ushma	–	–	–	All diseases
Sulphur	Katutikta	Ushma	Madhur	Pitta Kapha	–	All diseases.
Tamra }	Kasahya	Sheet	Madhur	Pitta Kapha	Guru Lekhana	Liver, Spleen
Bhasma }	Madhur					Kushtha, Aamvata
Abhrak }	Kashya	Sheet	Madhur	Tridosh		Spleen, Ascites
Bhasma }	Madhur					Kushtha, Poison, Wounds, Worms.
Loha }	Tikta	Sheet	Madhur	Tridosh	Guru	Anaemia, Kshaya.
Bhasma }	Kashya				Lekhana	Kushtha, All diseases.
Gulwel	Katu, Tikta	Ushma	Madhur	Tridosh	Laghu	Cough, Jaundice, Anaemia, Kushtha.

CHAPTER 17

USE OF AMRUTADIGUGGUL IN ACNE VULGARIS

Dr. V.V. Bhagwat

Introduction

Some teenagers get small pimples on the face around 16 years of age. Pus formation takes place in them if they are prickled by nails because of which face become ugly. That causes inferiority complex in some teenagers.

According to modern science the reason for 'pimples' is harmonal imbalance. In modern science treatment for pimples includes oral intake of antibiotics along with which care should be taken that the face does not remain oily. Some doctors also prescribe different ointment for local application.

The action of antibiotics is quite fast in some patients while in some patients pus formation takes place again after some days. To avoid that the course of anti–biotics should be continued for many days, some times as long as upto 1–1.5 months.

Side effects of long–term course of antibiotics such as indigestion, hyper acidity etc., are seen. These side effects can be avoided by Ayurvedic medicines.

Many medicines have been told in Ayurveda for mukh–dushika from which I have selected Amrutadiguggul for my experiment.

The 'patha' (formula) of Amrutadi Guggul is from the first 'Khanda' (Chapter) of Bharat Bhaishjya Ratnavali and its number is 133. This 'path' is initially from Bhaishajya Ratnavali. It is as follows :

Gulvel, Small Elaichi, Vavdinga, Kutaja Tvak, Indrajava, Harada, Aola and Guggul are to be taken in the proportion of 1 : 2 : 3 : 4 : 5 : 6 : 7 : 8 in the given order and all these herbal medicines are to be mixed in guggul. This medicine, when taken with honey cures pimples, fattiness and bhagandar (fistula).

Experiment

While preparing guggul Kalpas it is given that guggul and churpos should be mixed and triturated after which tablets should be made. For practical purpose water was mixed in guggul in which churnas were mixed and after the mixture had dried, tablets were prepared.

While using amruta guggul on pimples local application of any lep was not done. The patient was told to wash his mouth twice a day with chana–atta (chick pea powder) and luke-warm water.

Dosage

6 tablets of amrutadiguggul twice a day. Total tablets–12.

Each tablet was of 200 mg which means that daily intake of the medicine was 2400 mg. Some patients found difficulty in taking 6 tablets at a time, hence they were advised to take 4 tablets thrice a day.

According to the reference of the 'Grantha' the tablets are to be taken with honey. But as practically it is difficult for the patients to triturate 6 tablets each time and take the medicine with honey. Only 2 patients took the medicine with honey while the rest of the patients took the tablets along with water.

Duration of Treatment

For this experiment I gave medicine to the patients for one month.

Observations

Totally 18 patients came to me for the treatment of pimples out of which 3 patients took medicine for 7 days after which they did not come for follow up. The reason for that is not known. It has not been known whether the patients have took medicine for even 7 days. These patients have not been considered in this paper. Those 15 patients who have regularly taken medicine for one month have been considered in this project.

Table 1

Female	*Male*
5	10

Table 2

	Distribution according to age	*Number of patients*
1.	17 years	5
2.	19 years	6
3.	20 years	3
4.	21 years	1

Table 3 : Table according to results obtained

1.	Good Results	5
2.	Medium Results	2
3.	General results	1
4.	No results at all	7

Table 4

Vehicle–Honey	2
Vehicle–Water	13

(*a*) While taking into consideration the overall result of the medicine, it was found that 5 patients got good results which means that 33% of the patients were cured completely. The pimples on their faces were completely gone and their skin became smooth.

(*b*) Two patients got medium results. Some pimples on their faces were gone completely, while oedema of some pimples was reduced, while some pimples remained as they were. But the pus from all the pimples was gone completely.

(*c*) One patient got general result. The size of the pimples on the lady's face was reduced, but the number of pimples remained as it was.

(*d*) Seven patients did not get any results at all. The complaints of these patients remained as they were before starting the treatment even after the completion of the treatment.

(*e*) All the 15 patients told that after the treatment had started their bowels were cleared regularly and that they felt a sense of well–being after bowles were cleared. They also said that they had solid stools.

(*f*) In the uses of amrutadi guggul it has been given that it cures fattiness. But as the weights of the patients had not been recorded before starting the treatment, this use of the medicine could not be judged.

Discussion

The description of Tarunya pitika in Sushrut Samhita is as follows : The pimples appear on the face in teenage which resemble the thorn of shalmali tree. They are caused by Kapha, Vata and Rakta and are termed as Mukhdushika.

The same shloka has been written in Madhav Nidan in Kshudra Rogas.

The following reference is from Ashtanga Sangraha.

Pimples on the face which resemble the thron of Shalmali tree and which are hard and contain fat in them are termed as Mukh–dushika.

The Bruhat–trayi, Laghu–trayi or any other Granthas do not have much references about Mukh–dushika. Some shlokas about the treatment are seen in Shshrut Samhita, Sharandhar Samhita etc.

No reference about the 'hetus' (causes) and 'Samprapti' (pathogenesis) of Mukhdushika are found in Ayurvedic Granthas. In my opinion there is 'Vaigunya' in the twacha sthan of the face because of which the Kapha Vata and Rakta dosh get dushit which cause 'strotorodh' and mukhdushika are created.

According to modern science the reasons for mukh-dushika are as follows :

Sebum production is predominently hormonally stimulated. Androgens stimulate the sebaceous gland secretions. The pituitary gland in particular the anterior has an important role in controlling sebaceous gland secretion.

The following 8 medicines are included in the 'path' of Amruta guggul. Gulvel, Small elaichi, Vavdinga, Kutaja Twak, Indrajava, Avla and Hirda.

This path contains 8 parts of guggul. Guggul is medohar and according to Vagbhatacharya, the mukhdushika contains Meda (Fat). Guggul is medhar and it also reduces oedema. Different pathas of guggul like Triphala guggul are used in the treatment of mukhdushika.

Though the 'gunas' (characteristics) of the drugs used in Ayurvedic Medicine differ individually, the gunas of their mixture are found to be different. For example, Amruta Guggul–Bharat Bhaishajya is used for skin diseases. But if these drugs are used in the same 'patha' then it is useful in hyper–acidity–1 Bharat Bhaishjya.

The integrated guna of the medicines used in this 'patha' acts on fattiness. Fistula and mukh–dushika which may be because of the drugs used in this path are deepana, pachana.

In this experiment, results have not been found according to the granthas, only 33% result has been obtained which may be because :

Dosage

Amruta–guggul in the dose of 2400 mg was given daily.

The dosage of other guggul Kalpas has been written more in the granthas. The dosage of Chandra Prabha has been written as 1 Tola which means 12 mg; 12000 mg; but still the dosage of Arogyavardhini is given as 1 'Bora' which is approximately 6000 mg. Now a days patients find it difficult to administer such a large dose, hence the dose is reduced. It is possible that dosage of Amruta Guggul given by me has been low dose.

Vehicle

According to Granthas, Amruta guggul should be taken with honey. But only 2 of my patients took the medicine with honey, which may be one of the reasons for not getting good results.

Diet Restrictions

There were no diet restrictions to the patients in this experiment. According to Vrudha Vaidyadhar, oily and spicy food should not be taken by the patients of mukh–dushika.

The less results obtained may be due to the reason that no diet restrictions were followed by the patients.

The number of patients was less in the experiment undertaken by me. It should be carried out on a more large scale.

This experiment should be carried out by increasing the dosage, with honey as vehicle and with proper diet restrictions.

Acknowledgement

I am thankful to Ayurved Rasashala for providing the medicines and also to Institute of Indian Medicine for their help.

I am also thankful to Dr. P.H. Kulkarni and my wife Mrs. Neela Bhagwat for their help.

REFERENCES

The following material was referred by me during the treatment of mukhdushika.

1. The role of Shankha Bhasma in the treatment of Mukhadushika *i.e.,* acne or pimples by Dr. Vivek Shanbag.
2. Acne Vulgaris and Ayurved Rasashala products by Dr. Prakash Paranjpe.
3. Mukhadushika and Sukshma Triphala by Dr. Sunita Kulkarni.
4. Mukhadushika and Shankha Bhasma vati by Dr. Talokar.
5. Thiostanin and wang vikar by Dr. B.B. Date.

Their Rasa Virya Vipak are as follows :

Name	*Rasa*	*Virya*	*Vipak*	*Guna*	*Doshaghnata*
1. Gulvel	Titak, Katu, Kashaya	Ushna	Madhur	Laghu	Tridosh
2. Small elaichi	Katu, Madhur	Sheeta	Katu	–	Pitta–Kapha
3. Vavdinga	Katu	Ushna	Katu	Raksha Laghu	Kapha–Vata
4. Katun Tvak	Katu, Tikta	Sheeta	Katu	Ruksha	Kapha–Pitta.
5. Indrajav	Tikta, Katu	Sheeta	Katu	Sor–Laghu	Kapha–Pitta.
6. Hirda	Kashaya, Amla, Madhur, katu	Ushna	Madhur	–	Tridosh.
7. Avla	Amla, Madhur Kashaya	Sheeta	Madhur	Laghu	Tridosh.
8. Guggul	Katu, Tikta	Ushna	Katu	–	Kapha, Vata.

CHAPTER 18

SKIN DISEASES AND RASASHALA PRODUCTS

Prof. Dr. B.K. Bhagwat

Introduction

Various skin disorders are sought in day to day clinical practice. To name a few, Commonly Occurring skin disorders are acne, eczema, urtcaria, Leuconderma, Pigmentaiton disorders, scabi.es, boils, ringworm infestation etc. Ayurveda Rasashala, the well established Ayurvedic drugs' manufacturer has a valid drug licence issued by the Government of India. The authenticity of each plant and mineral component used, is established by the quality control laboratory of the company by qualified chemist approved by the Food and Drug Administration. Ayurveda Rasashala is engaged in manufacturing quality products of Ayurveda since last sixty years. It manufactures the drugs, for various disorders of the health, more than one fifty formulations. Ayurveda rasashala prepares numerous drugs which are immensely useful in various Skin diseases. To name a few, Thiostanin and Sookshma Triphala in tablet form, Sariwadyasav and Chandanasav like asavas, Khadirarishtaan arishta, decoctions or quaths like Bhoonimbadi and Mahamanjishthadi quath, many formulations in tablet form like Arogyavardhini, kamadudha, Chandandivati, Pravalpishti, Shankhabhasma vati, Bhootabhirav ras, Sootashekhar and so on. Rasashala has also a wide range of drugs in skin diseases, to be used for external applications also paribhadra tail, Vranaropak and Shodhak tails, Bavchilep goli, Padadari malam etc. are all effective external applications.

As a beginning of assessment of these drugs in skin problems we started with Acne Vulgaris, a very common problem of the youth, for clinical evaluation of Shankha-bhasma Vati.

Acne vulgaris is a chronic inflammatory disorder of the pilosebaceous follicles, commonly sought in the clinical practice. Ayurveda describes acne as 'Tarunya Peetika, meaning that disease of the adolescence. It has been mentioned that Vata, Kapha doshas and rakta–meda dhatu is the cause of acne *i.e.,* tarunya peetika. A variety of drugs have been used since centuries in the Ayurvedic system of medicine to treat this ailment these agents are – Sookshma Triphala, Shankhabhasma Vati, Arogyavardhini, Chandraprabha vati etc. We understood that all these drugs are said to be effective in acne vulgaris, but clinical trials of them are few yet. So we undertook a small clinical trial of Shankhabhasma vati in the patients of acne vulgaris.

Materials and Methods

Compositions of Shankhabhasma vati is plain bhasma of shankha (Conch) 250 mg. The authenticity of which is established by the quality control laboratory of the company.

Clinical Studies

Twenty five patients with moderate acne were recruited at Nanal Hospital. Patients were selected on the basis of having moderate acne vulgaris of the face manifested by atleast ten papules or pustules and atleast five open or closed comedones. At the time of entry into the study, they were in good health and biochemically euthyroid and nondiabetic. None of them had any endocrinal disorder.

All medication systemic and/or topical, if any, were discontinued one week before entry into our study. Written consent and detailed clinical history was obtained from the patients. They were randomised in two groups.

Dosage

Medications were taken only orally two tablets three times daily. The treatment was continued for six weeks. Group one received Shankhabhasma vati and group two a placebo.

Clinical Evaluation

All patients were clinically assessed very fortnightly inflammatory and non–inflammatory lesions on the face were counted until the end of study. The group one, which received Shankhabhasma vati showed 35% reduction in lesions, whereas the group two–which received placebo showed very insignificant reduction in lesions. Group one had fifteen patients out of which one patient was a dropout–Group two which received placebo, had ten patients out of which four patients were dropouts.

Discussion

In the present study, Shankhabhasma vati was given to unselected patients of acne vulgaris, in group one. This group showed improvement in severity of both inflammatory and noninflammatory lesions. Shankhabhasma alleviates pitta-dosha and so is useful in hyperacidity, pepticulcer, acne (Dr. V.V. Bhagwat) Further work is needed to document acne lesions with facial photographs. (Dr. Prakash Paranjpe).

Whether Shankhabhasma vati have any antiseptic and/or anti-inflammatory action remains to be investigated. During and after six weeks drug therapy none of the patients showed any untoward effect.

Acknowledgements

Many thanks to Ayurveda Rasashala and Management of Nanal Hospital.

REFERENCES

1. Dr. V.V. Bhagwat. (A study of Shankha bhasma in the treatment of Hyperacidy–Ayurvedic Research papers, Part I, Edited by Dr. P.H. Kulkarni, Published by Ayurvedic Rasashala, Pune).
2. Dr. Prakash Paranjpe (Assessment of comparative efficiency of Ayurvedic combinations in the treatment of Acne vulgaris : A randomised clinical evaluation 'Ayurveda Patrika' Nov. 1993).

CHAPTER 19

USE OF SOOKSHMA TRIPHALA IN GENERAL PRACTICE

Dr. Mrs. S.V. Doiphode &
Prof. Dr. V.V. Doipode

Introduction

Those of use who enjoy the benefits of living in modern civilisation also suffer all its disadvantages : Pollution of air water and food by chemicals and radiation, pollution of our mind by noise and information overload, pollution of our humanness by automation, pollution of our emotions by loneliness, alienation and the breakdown of the family. Civilisation is quite a recent development in the human history, and as our societies become more complex, we move further away from the rise environment in which we evolved. With the enormous rise in population and the pace of life, every family member has to work inevitably, for his/her existence. So there is demand for the quicker remedies from the society, for which many a times though not safe and effective in long terms, antibiotic is the answer.

Ayurveda, the ancient medical system of India shows how body mind and spirit interactions can be predicted, balanced and improved to enable us to live gracefully, harmoniously and healthily. In day to day practice, the patients of upper respiratory tract infections fever, common colds, influenza, urinary tract infections and various skin diseases are commonly sought. Many a times, chemotherapeutic agents are not required, essentially in early stages. Due to self medication or in want of alternative safer remedies, still antibiotics have been issued to a large extent. We found this is the area, in which a safe, effective and alternative or complimentary drug of Ayurveda can be tried for. Hence we undertook a pilot clinical study of evaluate the efficacy of "Sookshma Triphala" a proprietary drug of Ayurveda Rasa-shala, Pune. This formulation is used in multifarous ailments and is found to be effective. In present study, we have randomly taken the patients of U.T.I., U.R.T.I., Influenza, Skin infections, Ophthalmic and E.N.T. diseases to evaluate the efficacy of Sookshma Triphala alone or in combination with other therapy.

Subjects and Methods

This study was conducted amongst the patients attending my clinic in O.P.D. In this pilot screening of Sookshma Triphala, patients suffering from various ailments *viz.*, URTI, UTI Skin disorder, ENT and Ophthalmic diseases were treated with Sookshma Triphala alone or as an adjuvant. The Dosage for adults was 2 to 4 tablets three times a day and in children 1 to 2 tablets three times a day for required duration. The duration of study was not constant in all the patients. As this study was a pilot screening we have not designed the rigid methodology like control group, agewise or diseasewise similarities and pathological investigations etc.

In all 102 patients were treated in this clinical study. Their diseasewise and symptomwise information is detailed in Table 1. The systemwise distribution is shown in Table 2.

The patients in this study entered into this trial willingly only after signing an informed written consent. These individuals continued to consume their usual diet and no modification of dietary programme was encouraged irrespective of their ailments. During this study, subjects underwent clinical assessment on biweekly basis. Their temperature, pulse rate, respiration rate and blood pressure was recorded on every visit. Untoward effects, if any, were asked and/or seen at the time of their clinical assessment. The results of each patient were noted on the case papers.

Results

"Sookshma Triphala" the single drug has multifarous actions and hence various indications. In this study, Sookshma Triphala when used as an adjuvant, showed to speed up the recovers in many cases especially URTI and skin diseases. The composition of Sookshma Triphala (Table 3) shows that it has Kajjali only 10 mg, but the major portion is of triphala. So this composition though called as herbo–mineral, it has major herbal share. The role of Kajjali is to enhance the bioavailability of the drug. This action was concluded from this clinical study as the other drugs used in this study were sufficient on minimal dosages.

Discussions

'Shookshma Triphala' is recommended formulation in the skin disease, ophthamic ailments, as a blood purifier etc. From various other clinical trials and studies on Sookshma Triphala, it can be concluded that Sookshma Triphala has mild antibacterial, antiviral, and antiinflammatory actions. It must be increasing the body resistance in general. For repeated chronic infections like tonsilities, cold and sore throat, this drug will be the safest drug of first choice. In recurring Acne vulgaris, Sookshma Triphala can be used as it is the safest drug for even long term duration. 'Sookshma Triphala' can be used as a preventive drug in many common ailments like tonsillitis, acne, sinustis, stye, influenza etc. in day to day practice.

Elaborate study on different diseases with a control group is required to assess 'Sookshma Triphala' with scientific parameters. 'Sookshma Triphala' in future, is going to have its own place in practice for its safety and efficacy.

Acknowledgement

We thank 'Ayurved Rasashala', Pune for sponsoring the project, 'Institute of Indian Medicine' for references.

REFERENCES

1. Dr. U. Sudrik, Dr. S.A. Bhagli, Dr. V.B. Bhagli–"Management of style with Sweden and 'Sookshma Triphala'.
2. Dr. V.V. Doiphode, Dr. N.V. Bhave–"Dacryocystitis and Sookshma Triphala".
3. Dr. Avinash Lele, Dr. S.G. Joshi–"Use of Sookshma Triphala in Post tonsillectomy patients".
4. Dr. A. Kaid, Dr. P.H. Kulkarni–"Sookshma Triphala skin diseases."
5. Dr. Sunita Kulkarni, Dr. Karambelkar–"Sookshma Triphala in Acne."
6. Dr. Dilip Bhusari, Dr. V.V. Doiphode–"Sookshma Triphala and Style."
7. Dr. Shubhada Bopegamage–"To assess antiviral activity of Sookshma Triphala."
8. Dr. Prakash Paranjpe, Dr. P.H. Kulkarni–"Comparative efficacy of four Ayurvedic formulations in the treatment of Acne Vulgaris: A double blind randomized placebo controlled clinical evaluation.
9. Dr. Prakash Paranjpe–Clinical evaluation of mahamanjishthadi Quath and Sookshma Triphala in the Treatment of Acne Vulgaris.

Table 1 : Patients and their Treatment Schedule
ST : Sookshma Triphala

Sr.No.	*Symptoms*	*No. of Cases*	*Treatment*	*Duration (Days)*
1.	Fever, cough Rhinorrhoea	120	S.T. Aspirin, Tribhuvankirti CPM	03
2.	URTI	022	S.T.T. Kirti Aspirin	03
3.	Purulent discharge from eyes and malaise	004	S.T. Aspirin	07
4.	Frequency and burning of micturition	004	S.T. Cystone	05
5.	Boils	028	S.T. Aspirin Vit 'C'	05
6.	Skin infection	001	Tropical Cream.	05
7.	Acute Sinusitis	006	S.T. Aspirin	05
8.	Ringworm infestion	002	S.T. Gricioderm	10
9.	Lecuorrhoea, itching Vulva	002	S.T.Lukol	05
10.	Infected wound	002	S.T. Dressing	04
11.	Fever, cough Backache	002	S.T.T.Kirti	10
12.	Otitis external	002	S.T.C.P.M.	03
13.	Urticaria	002	S.T.C.P.M.	03
14.	Scabies	006	S.T.C.P.M. Sulphur	07

Table 2 : Systemwise Distribution of the patients
S.T. : Sookshma Triphala

Sr.No.	*Symptoms*	*No. of Cases*	*Treatment*	*Duration (Days)*
1.	Respiratory	144	S.T.Tribhuvan Kirti, Aspirin Chlorphena-raminamateate	3–10
2.	Urogental	006	S.T.Cystone Lukol	05
3.	Skin	042	S.T.Topical Point. Dressing Aspirin C.P.M., Sulphur Vitamin 'C'	3–10
4.	Ophthalmic	004	S.T. Aspirin	07
5.	Ear, Nose	008	S.T. Aspirin, C.P.M.	3–5

Table 3 : Composition of "Sookshma Triphala"

Sr. No.	*Local Name*	*Scientific Name*	*Plant Parts*	*wt. per tablet*
1.	'Sookshma Triphala' (250 mg. tablet)			
2.	Hirda	Terminalia Chebula Retz (Combretaceae)	Dried fruit	66.66
3.	Beheda	Terminalia Belerica Roxb (Combretaceae)	Dried fruit	66.66
4.	Amalaki	Emblica Officinalis Goerth (Euphorbiaceae)	Dried fruit	66.66
5.	Parad	Mercury pure	Mineral	5.0
6.	Gandhak	Sulphur pure	Mineral	5.0

CHAPTER 20

USE OF PADADARI IN PLANTER HYPER–KERATOSIS (FISSURED SOLES)

Prof. Dr. Jayant K. Barde

Introduction

Skin is a specialised tissue evolved to perform different functions in animals.

The structure of human skin differs in different places and organs, according to the functions it has to perform.

The soles of the feet are bearing maximum burden of the body and have maximum frictions, as it the only organ facing the surface, while standing and walking.

In Indian population many persons are found to be having Fissures on the sole of foot.

This is mainly found in the manual workers. Villagers, women and in lower and economics Strata. The cause apparently is walking without foot wear and exposure to dry weather and dust.

The tendency of most of the people is to ignore it till the condition becomes unbearable. Even then due to the large number of people suffering from this condition, many have to seek some remedy or the other. Hence we find many remedies being advertised to be of use against this connection. *E.g.* Crack, Amrut Malam, Kailas Jeevan etc.

Considering the intensity of the problem, a clinical trials of one preparation of Rasashala namely 'Padadari' for this condition was undertaken by me. This trial termed as 'Use of PADADARI' in planter Keratosis'.

Padadari

It is proprietory preparation of Ayurveda Rasashala. It contains following ingredients per 1 gm.

1.	Tankan (Dehydrated and Roasted Borax)	45 mgs.
2.	Kalkhapari (Carbonate of Zinc)	70 mgs.
3.	Sarjaras (Ral.) (Gum Resin of Shorea Robusta)	6 mgs.
4.	Narikel Tail (Cocos Neuciferra Oil)	20 mgs.
5.	Vaseline as Base	Q.S.

It is not a compound described in any of the old texts and who has evolved this formula is not clearly known.

Tankan–Borax (Na_2 B^{407})

Is known to be midly antiseptic, Local sedative and it relives itching.

Kalkhapri

It is a mineral containing Zn CO_3. It is purified by boiling in Cow's urine for 7 days and then used after words. It is used in skin diseases and itching, from Ayurvedic point of view.

Zinc forms an essential part of Enzyme system and is useful in wound healing.

Sarjaras

It is astringent, bactericidal and bacteriostatic. It has sealing activity along with other substances it is described as having wound healing properties. The Ayurvedic texts mention its use in wounds, "Vipadica" (Hyper Keratosis) and as having healing properties. ("Bhagna Sandhankar") and anti infective ("Bohoothanta").

Narikel Tail

It is unctus, soothing, relieves pain. It is "Vat and Pitta Shamak".

It has antifungal activity.

Material and Methods

A special camp was held for the treatment of the cracked feet. All the patients attending the camp were treated with "Padadari Ointment". In addition to that many other patients afterwards were also treated with the Ointment.

Special Examination form was prepared for keeping the record.

Most of the patients were chronic sufferers, and had used many other remedies. The duration of the complaint and the prior medication for the same were recorded.

Patients were examined at 7 days interval for 4 weeks, and the record was kept.

Some of the patients were photographed to show and prove the improvement visually. The patients suffering from concommittment diseases like fungal infestation, Diabetes, were not excluded from the treatment.

Those patients who did not complete the treatment of 4 weeks were eliminated form the trial.

The patients were advice to wash, clean and dry the feet and then apply sufficient quantity of the ointment to the affected part, two times a day.

All the cases selected for the study were adults. The age range being 18 yrs. to 72 yrs.

No differentiation as males and females was made while giving the treatment.

As a comparison and to judge the efficiency of the preparation, every fifth patient, irrespective of age, sex, severity etc. was given only vaseline for application.

Thus there were two groups :

1. Group "A"–treated with "padadari" comprised of 87 patients.
2. Group "B"–comprised of 21 patients, treated with vasaline.

The patients were specially examined for :

(*i*) Cracks.

(*ii*) Fissures.

(*iii*) Pain.

(*iv*) Tenderness.

(*v*) Inability to walk.

(*vi*) Bleeding.

(*vii*) Pus formation.

These were graded as 0, 1, 2, 3 according to severity. Thus :

"0" – No sign/symptoms

"1" – Mild symptoms.

"2" – Moderate Symptoms.

"3" – Severe Symptoms.

After each weekly examination the severity of each sign/symptoms was noted.

Self assessment by patient and subjective improvement were also considered for final assessment, which was graded as below :

Totally cured	+ 4
Marked improvement	+ 3
Moderate improvement	+ 2
Slight improvement	+ 1
No Change	0
Excerbations	– 1

Observations and Results

It is seen that in urban population more women suffer from fissured feet than men.

In the group 'A' beneficial effect of 'padadari' is slightly seen at the end of the 4th week.

More than 75% of the patients show marked improvement by the end of the 4th week. (It is further seen that continuing the preparation for further period, improvement continues in patients, who are not completely cared).

The time for improvement is dependent on the depth of the fissures and as such, those having deep fissures, take more time.

Since most of the patients had used one or the other preparations previously, they almost form a control group by themselves, thus proving the efficiency of "padadari Ointment".

Group B

In this group some of the patients showed some improvement, which at the end of the period of 4 weeks could not be said to be 30%.

This shows that there is significant improvement by using "Padadari Ointment" as compared with vasaline.

Some of the patients treated in this trial had Keratoderma, Atopic Dermatitis and Fungal infestation with or without diabeties. All of them showed moderate to marked improvement. The fissured soles are seen more in "Vat –, Pitta –, and Vat–Pitta" Prakruti Persons.

It is commonly seen to exacerbate in dry and dusty conditions, and in winter and summer, individuals showing personal variations.

Side Effects

There were no side effect seen or complaints by the patients, about the preparation. It is totally nonirritant. None at the patients showed any adverse skin reaction.

Conclusion

Fissuring of the sole is common skin disorder affecting a large member of Persons. At times it is so severe that it causes severe discomfort and disability. There could be bleeding and infection also.

There are many traditional, Ayurvedic and modern medical preparations showing variable improvement in the condition.

"Padadari Ointment" of Rasashala shows marked improvement in fissured soles. It appears to be of use when other remedies did not show improvement. It was also useful in certain cases of fungal infections and Atopic Dermatitis. The effect appears to be due to the :

1. Barrier Action of the preparation.
2. Wound healing properties described in Ayurvedic Texts.
3. Anti–infective and Anti–Fungal activity.

Acknowledgement

I thank the management of Vd. Purshottam Shastri Nanal Rugnalaya for providing the facilities for this trials.

I sincerely thank Dr. Pradeep Mahajan (Hon. Dermatologist–Nanal Hospital) for his valuable guidance and suggestions.

I also thank Ayurveda Rasashala for providing free samples of "Padadari Ointment" for the use of the patients and for the financial support.

I thank the staff of the employees of Vd. Purushottam Shastri Nanal Hospital for helping me in carrying out this project.

Comments

Apparently the disease Vipadika, or padadari is produced by the vitiating of the dosha vata. It could be said to be caused by the lessening of 'Sneha (oil) and Jala (water)', The attributes of 'Kapha' dosha which are essential for binding activity and continuity of the tissues and maintenance of life force, lusture, etc.

However, the fluid property of 'Jal' is the one which hampers the healing process, in which wound (discontinuity in the tissue) is to be kept dry and clean (Ruksha and vishad) and devoid of 'Kleda'.

Certain unctous substances have healing properties, certain unctous substances are apparently unctous, but from Ayurvedic point of view are dry (Ruksha) *e.g.*, Vasaline.

Certain substances have peculiar pharmocological action specific to that substances only, known in Ayurvedic as 'Prabhav' (special effect). The 'Rasa' 'Kashay' (astringent) has drying effect, hence it is of use in wound healing.

The action may be of protective nature due to inert substances, held together by the vehicle, thus forming a barrier.

The vehicle vaseline is non–absorbable, sticky and messy, due to which dust and other things adhere to it. This may hamper the therapeutic effect. Also it is not an 'Ayurvedic' substance.

Instead of that bees–wax or wax can be used with advantage. Also the 'Kokam Oil' can be used. It is also a mild antiseptic and antifungal agent.

A modern type of cream can also be prepared, which will be cosmetically, acceptable and pharamacologically advantageous.

Better results may be obtained if the zinc content of Kalkhapari is more.

Table 1 : Gradation of Patients According to Severity

	No. of Fissure and Cracks		*Depth Fissures*		*Pain*		*Bleeding*	
	Gr A	Gr B	Gr A	Gr B	Gr A	Gr B	Gr A	Gr B
							80	
Absent	–	–	17	4	12	4	–	18
Mild	28	8	30	10	57	13	1	2
Moderate	41	10	22	4	12	2	6	1
Severe	18	3	18	3	6	2	0	0

Table 2 : Response to Therapy–Group B

Clinical Features	*Grading Scale*	*Patient Distribution on Grading Scale*				
		Per-treat-ment	*On 7th day*	*On 14th day*	*On 21st day*	*On 28th Day*
No. of Fissures and Cracks	0	0	0	0	2	4
	18	9	12	11	9	
	2	10	9	7	6	6
	3	3	3	2	2	2
Depth of Fissures	0	4	5	8	8	10
	1	10	10	8	8	7
	2	4	3	3	3	3
	3	3	3	2	2	1
Pain	0	4	6	10	11	11
	1	13	11	8	8	8
	2	2	2	2	1	1
	3	3	2	1	1	1
Bleeding	0	18	18	20	21	21
	1	2	2	1	–	–
	3	–	–	–	–	–
Side Effect	0	–	–	–	–	–
	1	–	–	–	–	–
	2	–	–	–	–	–
	3	–	–	–	–	–

Table 3 : Response to Therapy–Group A

Clinical Features	*Grading Scale*	*Patient Distribution on Grading Scale*				
		Per-treat-ment	*On 7th day*	*On 14th day*	*On 21th day*	*On 28th Day*
No. of Fissures and Cracks	0	0	4	18	4	2
	28	33	51	49	3	5
	2	41	38	22	15	8
	3	18	16	10	5	2

(Contd...)

Clinical Features	*Grading Scale*	*Patient Distribution on Grading Scale*				
		Per-treat-ment	*On 7th day*	*On 14th day*	*On 21th day*	*On 28th Day*
Depth of Fissures	0	17	22	42	57	68
	1	30	31	20	16	10
	2	22	20	18	10	7
	3	18	14	7	4	2
Pain	0	12	42	59	76	80
	1	57	31	20	6	4
	2	12	10	6	4	2
	3	6	4	2	1	1
Bleeding	0	80	82	85	87	87
	1	1	2	2	–	–
	2	6	3	–	–	–
	3	–	–	–	–	–
Side Effects	0	87	87	87	87	87
	1	–	–	–	–	–
	2	–	–	–	–	–
	3	–	–	–	–	–

CHAPTER 21

CLINICAL STUDY OF DC TABLETS (GHANASAR OF INGREDIENTS OF KHADIRARISHTA, SARIVADYASAVA AND MAHAMANJISHTHADI KWATH OF AYURVEDA RASASHALA) IN VARIOUS SKIN PROBLEMS

Prof Dr. P.H. Kulkarni

Introduction

Medical practitioners come across various skin disorders in day to day medical practice. Many preparations are advocated in Ayurvedic Literature.

It was decided to prepare and use Ghanasara (Solid water extracts) of ingredients of Khadirarishta, Sarivadhyasava and Mahamanjishthadi Kwath manufactured by Ayurveda Rasashala pune (India) in various skin disorder.

Methodology

A. (*i*) Ingredients of Khadirarishta, Sarivadyasava and Mahamanjishtadi Kwath were boiled in water till all water evaporates, Mixture was kept stirred constantly to avoid charring. Tablets weighing 250 mgms were prepared.

B. (*i*) 2 tablets of DC were orally administered 3 times a day with a sip of water.

(*ii*) Patients were selected on random basis at out–patient department without consideration of age, sex, occupation, prakruti (Constitution) etc.

(*iii*) Patients were examined every week and observations were recorded.

(*iv*) DC Tablets were also used in patients at Australia, Newzealand and some European countries. However these patients are not considered in this study.

C. (*i*) Ingredients of DC ghanasar tablets are Sariwa, Manjishtha and Khadira.

(*ii*) DC tablets contains 37 plants.

(*iii*) Rasa (Taste) of tablet–Tikta–27 plants

Kashaya (Astringent)–18 plants

Katu (Pungent)–17 plants

(*iv*) Veerya (Protency).

Ushna (Hot)–24 ingredients

Sheet (Cold)–13 ingredients

(*v*) Vipaka (Post digestive effect)

Katu–30

Madhur (sweet)–04

(*vi*) 24 ingredients are Ruksha (dry) and Laghu (Light) in nature.

Observations

Age wise

1.	0–10	04
2.	11–20	20

(Contd...)

3. 21–30	07
4. 31–40	11
5. 41–50	03
6. 50–60	04
7. 61–70	01

Sex wise

Male	33
Female	17

Occupations

1. Service	01
2. Artist	01
3. Household	05
4. Student	23
5. Service	11
6. Teacher	03
7. Tinmaker	01
8. Retired	01
9. Business	03
10. Farmer	01
	50

Prakruti

1. Vata Pitta	18
2. Pitta Vata	21
3. Pitta Kapha	09
4. Kapha Pitta	—
5. Vata Kapha	01
6. Kapha Vata	01

Symptoms

1. Pruritus	09.
2. Vitilito	03
3. Discoloration	07
4. Pigmeutadian	02
5. Urticaria	06
6. Boils	08
7. Dermatitis	07
8. Acne	07
9. Eczema	12

Number of Days

Days	*No. of Patients*
1. 14	22
2. 28	28
Total	50

Relief

1. Moderate (30%)	:	05	10%
2. Good (60%)	:	13	26%
3. Excellent (80%)	:	32	64%
		50	

Discussion

1. 40% skin problems observed in the age group of 11–20 years.
2. Students formed a large group *i.e.,* 46% in this study.
3. Vata Pitta and Pitta vata constitution patients having largest group *i.e.,* 78%.

4. All patients were symptoms free within 2–4 weeks. Urticaria, Boils were corrected within few weeks and eczema, dematitis required 4 weeks.
5. 80% or more relief was observed in 64% of patients.
6. DC Tablets were administered to unselected patients.
7. It seems that DC Tablets corrects Dosha Vitiation.

Conclusion

DC tablets are useful in skin disorders and are also safe and economical to the patients.

Acknowledgement

Thanks are due to Ayurveda Rasashala, Pune (India) for sponsoring the project and Institute of Indian Medicine for providing the research facilities and references.

REFERENCES

1. Kulkarni P.H.–Ayurveda for you, Sagar Prakashan, Pune–29 (India) 1999.
2. Kulkarni and Palkar–Ayurvediya Aushadhi, Ayurveda Rasashala, Pune (India) 1995.
3. Kulkarni P.H. "Clinical assessment of mixture of Khadirarishta, Mahamanjishthadi Kwath and Sarivadyasava in the subtle form *i.e.,* DC 3 X Globules in various skin disorders". Ayurveda Research Papers II, Ayurveda Rasashala, Pune (India) 1995.

CHAPTER 22

CLINICAL ASSESSMENT OF 'KHASAM' (A MIXTURE OF KHADIRARISHTA + SARIWADYASAV + MAHAMANJISHTHADI QUATH) OF AYURVED RASASHALA IN COMMON SKIN DISEASES

Dr. Prof. K.V. Shah

Summary

Twenty eight patients with common Skin Problems were randomly treated with one mixture called "Khasam" liquid, orally for the duration of four weeks. The patients with skin diseases like Acne, dermatitis, eczema, boils, vitiligo, discolouration of skin, urticaria were incorporated in the study. Results were assessed by Counting the reduction in their lesions in 3 grades *viz.* moderate 30%, Good 60% and excellent 80% alongwith the relief they had. This mixture 'Khasam' was well tolerated.

Introduction

Acne, eczema, dermatitis, vitiligo, urticaria etc. are the commonly sought problems of the skin in daily practice. Treating these conditions has a problem, of the skin in daily practice. Treating these condition has become a problem, since safe drugs are not available. Systemic and topical antibiotics have been used for a long time thought they are not completely free from adverse effects.

In treating ance, the use of clindamycin may cause pseudombranous colitis (Milestone *et. al.* 1981), tetracycline may colour the skin yellow and erythromycin may precipitate hepatic disorders (Coskey 1975) though effective, isoretinion causes untoward effects with great frequency including risk of teratogenicity (Lammer *et al.* 1985). Thus there is a clear need for a safer and effective drug for long term therapy of acne vulgaris. Similarly treating eczema has become a problem as many a times topical as well as orally the steroids become necessary. In prutitus and urticaria, the treatment incorporates antihistaminws which show untoward effects like drowsyness etc. Hence there is a clear need for a safer and effective drug for long term therapy of these common skin disorders.

According to principles of Ayurveda, agnimandya *i.e.,* decreased appetite leads to faulty digestion and absorption, which results in formation of 'ama' this 'ama' deranges the tissue transformation brief, the derangement of dhatu formation, Vitiation of doshas, production of ama and kleda play a vital role in the aetilogy of skin diseases. The mixture 'Khasam' is a mixture of three very commonly used drugs in the skin diseases *viz.,* Khadirarishta, Sarivadyasava and Mahamanjishthadi Quath out of which, Khadirasishta is an excellent drug in eczema, scabies, ringworm infestations alongwith many other skin disorder. It is more useful in skin diseases with Kapha dosha vitiation.

(Bahrat Bhaishaj Ratnakar)

Sarivadyasav (Bharat Bhaishaj Ratnakar) is especially useful in skin diseases with diabetes mellitus. This asav alleviates pitta symptoms like burning–sensation in the body. Mahamanjishtadi Quath is a decoction commonly used as a blood purified by Ayurvedic physicians. It alleviates the symptoms of pitta and kapha dosha mainly hotness and pruritus. It is also useful in the treatment of discolouration of the skin, suppuration, depigmentation etc. (Bharat Bhaishaj Ratnakar). In the present study, we have used the combination of above three drugs called 'Khasam'. The effect of the combination of these three well known drugs have not been tested in clinical trials. Therefore we undertook a randomised clinical trial in commonly sought skin diseases in clinical practice.

Materials and Method

Ayurvedic medicine 'Khasam'–a mixture of three drugs is detailed in Table 1, 2 and 3 was obtained from Ayurveda rasashala of pune, a well establish company. The authenticity of each plant was established by the Quality Control Laboratory of the company by qualified chemist approved by F.D.A.

Clinical Studies

Twenty eight patients, of which 19 male and female patients between the age of 5 and 55 years with skin problems like acne, eczema, dermatitis, Vitiligo, urticaria, boils, pruritus (distribution–Table 4) were treated with oral 'Khasam' in the dose of 20 ml. three times a day, for the duration of 4 weeks. Physical examination was done at every weekly interval. Written consent was taken on the entry into the study with their signature. The patients were asked to withdraw the treatment if any, for their skin problems.

Clinical Evaluation

The patients attended for clinical evaluation at weekly

interval. The evaluation was made in two types. One with regression of their skin lesions and the other with regression of their symptoms from their history. The gradation of result was done as per relief of their symptoms *viz.*, 30% relief Moderate, 60% relief–Good and more than 80% relief excellent.

Result

Twenty seven patients completed the study and there was only one dropout during the course of the study. Out of twenty seven patients, moderate results were obtained in 4 patients, good results were obtained in 10 patients and excellent results were obtained in 13 patients.

Discussion

In the present study, one drug 'Khasam' was given to unselected patients of various skin problems. It appears that 'Khasam' reduces the severity of skin problems and improvement in their symptoms. The treatment with 'Khasam' did not produce any significant changes in other clinical parameters like pulse rate, body temp. etc., The exact mechanism of 'Khasam' cannot be documented from our study. It seems that this drug may be alleviating the kleda dushti and vitiation of doshas. Further clinical trials with control on each skin disease is wanted. The drug 'Khasam' was well tolerated.

Conclusion

'Khasam' was found to be effective in mainly kapha–pitta constitutions predominently.

Acknowledgement

We thank Ayurveda Rasashala, for providing the drug 'Khasam' for this clinical trial and Institute of Indian Medicine for references and research facilities.

REFERENCES

1. Milstone E.B. Mc Donald A.J., Scholhamer C.F. (1981) Pseddo-membranous colitis after topical application of clindamycin. Archives of Dermatitis 117, 154–155.
2. Coskey R.J. (1975) Side effects of antibiotics, therapy in acne vulgaris, Cutis 15, 710–712.
3. Lammer E.J. (1985) Retinoic acid embryopathy. New England Journal of medicine, 313, 837–841.
4. Bharat Bhaishaj Ratnakar–Khadirarishta–1096.
5. Bharat Bhaishaj Ratnakar–Sariwadyasava–7438.
6. Bharat Bhaishaj Ratnakar Mahamanjishthadi Quath–4979.
7. Kulkarni P.H. clinical assessment of Mixture of Khadirarishta, Mahamanjishthadi Kwath and Sarivadyasava in the subtle from *i.e.*, DC 3X Globules in various skin disorders. Ayurveda Research papers II Ayurveda Rasashala, 1995.

Table 1 : Composition : Khadirarishta

Local Name	*Weight/10 ml Volume (in mg.)*
Khadir sal	1000
Triphala	400
Bavachi	250
Kankol	20
Elaichi	20
Dalchini	20
Tejapatra	20
Lendi Pimpli	80
Deodar	400
Daruhald	500
Madha	4000
Lavanga	20
Jayphal	20
Mire Kale	20
Nagkeshar	20

Table 2 : Composition : Sariwadyasav

Local Name	*Weight/10 ml Volume (in mg.)*
Sariwa	20
Lodhra	20
Pimpalsal	20
Anantmool	20
Pahadmool	20
Gulvel	20
Owa	20
Koshtha	80
Hirda	80
Vala	20
Chhoti Elaichi	80
Nagarmotha	20
Vata sal	20
kachora	20
Padmakashtha	20
Amalaki	20
Raktachanadan	20
Kutki	20
Sonamukhi	80
Manuka	1200
Shweta Chandan	20
Badi Elaichi	80

Table 3 : Composition : Mahamanjishthadi Quath

Local Name	*Weight/10 ml Volume (in mg.)*
Manjishtha	Kadunimb sal
Adulasa	Triphala
Chitrak	Halad
Daruhalad	Gulvel

(Contd...)

Local Name	*Weight/10 ml Volume (in mg.)*	
Kadechirait	Rakta Chanda	All
Khair Sal	Kutki	100 mg.
Bavchi	Amlavetas	each
Morwel	Dantimool	
Indrayan	Vavding	
Jatamansi	Traymana	
Pahad Mool	Nishottar	
Anant Mool	Kadu Padwal	
Mire	Pimpli	

Table 4 : Distribution of Diseases

Disease	*No of Patients*
Eczema	8
Dermatitis	3
Acne Vulgaris	2
Vitiligo	1
Urticaria	7
Dyspigmentation	7

CHAPTER 23

ASSESSMENT OF COMPARATIVE EFFICACY OF AYURVEDIC COMBINATIONS IN THE TREATMENT OF ACNE VULGARIS : A RANDOMISED CLINICAL EVALUATION

Dr. Prakash Paranjpe &
Prof. Dr. P.H. Kulkarni

Abstract

Acne Vulgaris, a chronic inflammatory disorder of the pilosebaceous follicles, is an important disorder in clinical practice Treating acne has become a problem since safe drugs are not available for long term therapy.

Ayurveda describes acne vulgaris as 'Tarunya Peetika' meaning a disease adolescence. A clinical trial was taken on 25 patients of acne in Kolhapur for the duration of 6 weeks. Five Ayurvedic formulations of Ayurveda Rasashala, Pune were given in combinations and in five groups inflammatory lesions on the face. Facial photographs were taken initially at the end of the study.

Introduction

Acne vulgaris, a chronic inflammatory disorder of the

pilosebaceous follicles is an important disorder commonly sought in the clonical practice. The last ten years have seen several versies persist. The introduction of more effective, regiment of oral antibiotic therapy and the advent of oral retinoids have transformed the control of this disease. Still, treating once has become a problem since safe drugs are not available for long term therapy. The use of clindamycin may cause pseudomembranous colitis (Milestone *et. al.,* 1981), tetracyelin may causes the skin yellow and erythomycine may precipitate hepatic disorders (Coskey 1975). Though effective isotretinoin cause upward effect including risk of teratogenicity (Lammer *et. al*; 1985) there is a clear need for a safer drug for long term therapy once vulgaris. Ayurveda is the ancient science of life Sushruta has mentioned distinctively the seven layers of the skin *viz*., Avabhasini, Lohita, Shweta, Tamra, Vedini, Rohini and Mamswadhara respectively (Sushrut Samhita 1985) Ayurveda has claimed the acne vulgaris (Tarunya Peetika) to be due to derengement in third and fourth layer of skin due to vitiation of Vata and Kapha doshas and Rakta and meda dhatus.

A variety of drugs have been used since centuries in the Ayurvedic system of medicine to treat this condition. These agents are Sookshma Triphala, Shankhbhasma vati, Chandraprabhavati are claimed to be safe and effective (Sharangdhar Samhita 1984). Therefore we understood a randomise clinical trial of these agents singly and in combinations in the treatment of acne vulgaris.

Materials and Methods

Composition of the four formulation are detained in table I and were obtained from well established company, Ayurved Rasashala, Pune, which has a valid drug licence issued by the Government. The authenticity of each plant and mineral component was established by the quality control laboratory of the Company by qualified chemist approved by the Food and Drug administration.

Clinical Studies

Twenty five patients between the ages 18 and 28 years with moderate acne were recruited at Konark Health Center, Kolhapur. Patients were selected on the basis of having moderate acne vulgaris of the face manifested by atleast 10 papules or pustules and at least 5 open or closed comedones. At the time of entry into the study, they were in good health and bio-chemically enthyroid and nondiabetic. None of them had any endocrinal disorder.

All topical and systematic acne treatment and medications, if any, were discontinued at least two weeks before entry into the study. Written informed consent and a detailed clinical history was obtained from the patients. They were randomised into five groups.

Dosage and Care Regimen

Medications were assessed clinically every two weeks.

Initially inflammatory and non-inflammatory lesions on face were counted until the end of study. Patients compliance was assessed by counting the tablets remaining in tablet container, returned by them every two weeks. Facial photographs were taken initially at the end of the study.

Results

Twenty patients completed the study and there were five dropouts during the course of the study. Five groups of five patients each were given different combinations (Table 2). In group one, only Sookshma Triphala was given, showed

30% reduction in the lesions, Group two, in which a herbal combination A-1 showed 80% reduction in lesions. In Group Three, Sookshma Tripala along with Herbal Combination. A-1 showed 85% reduction in the lesions. In Groups four, Sookshma Triphala with Shankhbhasmavati showed 35% reduction in lesions. In Group five, Sookshma Triphala and Chandraprabhavati showed 35% reduction in lesions.

Discussion

In the present study, Ayurvedic drugs were given to unselected patients of acne vulgaris. Group three and two showed significant improvement in severity of both inflammatory as well as non-inflammatory lesions. It appears that treatment with this Ayurvedic formulations reduced the severity of once and produces a clinically significant improvement. The exact mechanism of action of these Ayurvedic drugs cannot be documented from our study. Whether these drugs have any antiseptic and/or anti-inflammatory activity remains to be investigated. Further work is very much needed into invest the long term effect of these formulations. During and after six weeks drugs therapy none of the patients showed any side effect.

Acknowledgement

We thank Ayurved Rasashala, Pune for sponsoring the drugs. Corporation from the management of Konark health Center, Kolhapur, deserves special thanks. Photographer Mr. Shailendra Ranade deserves special thanks too.

REFERENCES

1. Milestone E.E., McDonal A.J. Scholhamer C.F. (1981) Pseudomembranous colitis after topical application of clinadamycin. Archieves of Dermatology, 117, 154-155.

2. Coskey R.J. (1975) Side effect of antibiotic therapy in acne vulgaris, Cutis 15, 710-712.
3. Lammer E.J. (1985) Retinesic acid embroypathy. New England Journal of Medicine, 313, 837-841.
4. Marathi Sushrut Samhita (1985) Editor P.H. Kulkarni, Sagar Prakashan, Pune, Part 2, Page 111-112.
5. Sharangdhar Samhita (1984). Translated by K.K. Shrikant Murti, Chaukhamba Orienta, Varanasi, India, p. 82-85.

CHAPTER 24

ESTIMATION OF EFFICACY OF FOUR AYURVEDIC FORMULATIONS IN THE TREATMENT OF ACNE VULGARIS–A RANDOMISED CLINICAL EVALUATION WITH COMBINATIONS

Dr. Prakash Paranjpe
Nanal Hospital, Pune-4
Prof. Dr. P.H. Kulkarni
Director, Institute of Indian Medicine, Pune-411 029

Abstract

Acne Vulgaris, a chronic inflammatory disorder of the philosebaceous follicles, is a common disorder in clinical practice. Treating acne has become a problem since safe drugs are not available for long term therapy.

Ayurveda describes acne vulgaris as "Tarunya Peetika" meaning a disease of adolescence. A clinical trial was taken on 125 patients of acne at Pune for the duration 8 weeks. Four Ayurvedic formulation of Ayurvedic Rasashala, Pune were given in combination in five groups. No drug was given for topical application. Clinical evaluation was done by counting the inflammatory and non-inflammatory lesions on the face Facial photographs were taken initially and at the end the study.

Introduction

The last ten years have seen several exciting advances in understanding of acne, though several controversies persist. The introduction of more effective regimens of oral antibiotic therapy and the advent of oral retinoids have transformed the control of this disease. Treating acne has become a problem still, since safe drugs are not available for long term therapy. The use of clindamycin may cause pseudo-membranous colitis (milestone at 1981) tetracyclin may cause skin yellow and erythrocin may precipitate hepatic disorders (Coskey 1975). Though effective, Isotretnoin causes untowards effects including risk of tetratogenicity (Lammer *et al* 1985). There is a clear need for a safer drug for long term therapy of acne vulgaris. Since centuries, a variety of drugs have been used in the Ayurvedic system of medicine to treat this condition along with Sookshma triphala, a herbal composition named sundervati (designed by Dr. Prakash Paranjpe) Panchamrut Parpati and Amritadi Guggul were the four formulations used in combinations in this randomised clinical trial in the treatment of Acne Vulgaris.

Material and Method

Ayurvedic medicines compositions on the four formulations are detailed in Table were contained from Ayurveda Rasashala Pune.

Clinical Studies

One hundred and twenty five patients between 18 and 28 years with moderate acne were recruited patients were selected on the basis of having moderate acne manifested by atleast 5 open of closed comedones. At the time of entry they were in good health and biochemically enthyroid and non-diabetic. None of them had and endocrinal disorder.

All topical and systemic acne treatment and medications, if any, were discontinued at least two weeks before entry into the study. Written informed consent and detailed clinical history was obtained from the patients. They were randomised into five groups. Dosage and Care Regimen Medications were assessed orally two tablets three times daily. Patients were asked to wash their faces three times daily with milk soap. The treatment was continued for 8 weeks.

Clinical Evaluation

The patients were assessed clinically every two weeks initially every fortnightly inflammatory and non-inflammatory lesions were counted until the end of study. Patients compliance was assessed by counting the tablets remaining in the plastic container returned by them every two weeks Facial photographs were taken initially and at the end of study.

Result

Eighty nine patients completed the study and there were thirty six dropouts during the course of study. Five groups of twenty five patients each were given different combinations (Table 2). In Group A only Sookshma Triphala was given showed 30% reduction in the lesions Group B in which herbal combination Sundervati was given showed 75% reduction in the lesion in Group C combination of Sookshma Triphala and Sundervati was given. Which showed 80% reduction in the lesions. In Group D, Amritadi Guggul showed only 25% reduction in the lesions. In Group E a combination of Pravalpishti vati and Sundervati was given which showed 30% reduction in the lesions.

Discussion

In the present study Ayurvedic drugs were given in

unselected patients of acne vulgaris Group C and B showed significant improvement in severity of both inflammatory and non-inflammatory lesions. It appears that treatment with this Ayurvedic formulations reduces the severity of acne and produces a clinically significant improvement in acne. However treatment with other Ayurvedic formulations and combinations *viz*., Group A, D and E. Failed to show and significant clinical improvement (Table 3). The exact mechanism of action for these Ayurvedic drugs cannot be documented from our study. Whether these drugs have any antiseptic and or anti-inflammatory activity remains to be investigated. One clinical observation in the patients from Group [B, C and E] is quite interesting. The patients from these groups received decrease in the oilyness of their face suggesting the drugs may be decreasing the sebaceous secretions. Further work is very much needed to investigate the long term effects of these formulation. During and after eight weeks drug therapy none of the patients showed any side effects.

Acknowledgement

We thank Ayurveda Rasashala Pune for supply of the drugs.

REFERENCES

1. Milestone E.B. McDonald A.J. Scholhamler C.F. (1981) Pseudomembranous colitis after topical application of clindamycin. Archieves of Dermatology, 117 154-155.
2. Coskey R.J. (1975) side effects of antibiotics therapy in acne.

Table 1

S.No.	*Name*	*Ingredients*		*Weight per Tab (mg)*
1.	Sookshma Triphala	Mercury + Sulphur Purified (Kajjali)	08 mg.	250
		Triphala Powder	242 mg.	
2.	Sundervati	Kutaj bark	180 mg.	
		Amalaki	030 mg.	250
		Vidanga	010 mg.	
		Shunthi	13 mg.	
3.	Amritadi Guggul	Guduchi	13 mg.	
		patol	13 mg.	
		Shunthi	13 mg.	
		Marich	13 mg.	
		Pippal	13 mg.	250
		Haritaki	13 mg.	
		Bibhitak	13 mg.	
		Amalaki	13 mg.	
		Vidanga	117 mg.	
4.	Praval Pishti Vati	Praval Pishti	250 mg.	250

Table 2

Group 1	*Group 2*	*Group 3*	*Group 4*	*Group 5*
Sookshma Triphala	Sunder vati	Sookshma Triphla + Sundar Vati	Amritadi Guggul	Pravalpishti Vati +

Table 3

	Group A	*Group B*	*Group C*	*Group D*	*Group E*
No of Patients	25	25	25	25	25
Dropouts	07	04	06	11	06
Results :					
Excellent	01	06	08	00	01
Good	12	12	09	02	08
Fair	04	03	01	10	06
Poor	01	00	01	02	02

CHAPTER 25

SOME COMMON SKIN DISEASES AND THEIR TREATMENT

(SKIN DISEASES RELATED MOSTLY TO FACE AND COSMETIC PURPOSE HAVE ONLY BEEN CONSIDERED)

Dr. Manish Patwardhan

Skin Care Through Ayurvedic Cosmetology

One of the specialities of Ayurveda is that it not only says how to treat various ailments, but it also tells us about, how to remain free from ailments and healthy. These rules for the healthy person (Swastha) have been lead down in Dincharya (Daily routine) and Rutucharya (Routine to be followed in various seasons). In this respect special mention should be made to skin care. Following practises have been mentioned in the Dincharya for purpose of skin care.

1. Abhyanga (अभ्यङ्ग)

Applying oil to body especially to Head, Plantar area and Ears.

अभ्यङ्गमाचरेन्नित्यं स जराश्रमवातहा॥7॥
दृष्टिप्रसादपुष्ट्यायुः स्वप्नसुत्वक्त्वदार्ढ्यकृत्।

अष्टांगहृदय – सूत्रस्थान अ-2/श्लोक-7

One should apply oil to the body everyday. It keeps away aging, tiredness, vatadosha. It clears the vision (improves vision) increases life (आयुष्य).

Makes the skin soft, delicate and shining. Makes the body sturdy and builds up the body.

So for every day purpose for Abhayanga, Sessame oil (Til Tail) is the best but one can also use Olive Oil, Almond Oil etc. Medicated oil like Narayan tail or Chandanbalalakshadi Tail can also be used for this purpose.

2. Udvartana

Udvartana is applying Utane *i.e.,* external application of one or mixture of powders of various herbs which are said to be beneficial to skin (त्वच्य). This Utane is mixed with cold water/milk for dry skins and made into paste and then applied and then peeled off by rubbing.

Uses

उद्वर्तनं कफहरं मेदसः प्रविलापनम्।
स्थिरीकरणमङ्गानां त्वकप्रसादकरं परम्॥

अष्टांगहृदय–सूत्रस्थान अ–2/14

Application of utane decreases the Kapha dosha from the body, decreases the Meda dhatu (extra fats), makes the body sturdy, **makes the skin very clean.**

Other uses not mentioned in the verse but are found practically are :

1. It can be used to treat various skin diseases.
2. It acts as a deodorant.
3. It improves the quality and texture of skin and improves the complexion.

When instead of applying paste only dry powder is applied to the body. It is called **"Uddhulan"**.

3. Mukha Lepa

Various local applications have also been indicated for various common skin diseases and for skin care purpose in general for improving the complexion of skin, improving the tone of skin.

ग्रन्थ संदर्भ

(1) **जम्ब्वाम्रपल्लवा मस्तुहरिद्रे द्वे नवो गुडः।**
लेपः सवर्णकृत्पिष्टं.....................॥

अष्टांगहृदय–उत्तरस्थान 32/22

(2) **रक्तचंदनमंञ्जिष्ठाकुष्ठरोध्रप्रियङ्गवः।**
वटाङ्कूरा मसूराश्च व्यङ्गघ्ना मुखकान्तिदाः॥

अष्टांगहृदय–उत्तरस्थान 32/17

All the herbs explained in *Table* (*1*) are useful for this purpose.

SPECIALITY OF AYURVEDIC COSMETOLOGY

Ayurveda science has given detailed information for curing the faults caused after wound healing. It may be a post operative wound/or any wound as such.

Following methods have been explained for this purpose.

1. Savarnikarana

After a wound gets healed there remains a scar, this scar has got a lot of importance from cosmetic purpose and hence needs to be cured.

ग्रंथ संदर्भ–

लाक्षामनोह्वामञ्जिष्ठाहरितालनिशाद्वयैः।
लेपः सगोमयरयः सवर्णकरणः परम्॥

अष्टांगहृदय–उत्तरस्थान 25/62, 63

Local application of Laksha, Manaasheel, Manjishtha, Hartal, Haridra, Daruharidra made into paste in cowdung and applied on the scar, removes the scar.

2. Romasanjanan

Hairs generally do not grow on the scar. For this purpose

दग्धो वारणदन्तोन्तर्धूमं तैलं रसाञ्जनम्॥
रोमसञ्जननो लेपस्तद्वतैलपरिप्लुता।
चतुष्पाद् नखरोमास्थित्वक्शृंगखुरजा मषी॥

अष्टांगहृदय–उत्तरस्थान 25/62, 63

Antardhoom mashi (black ash) of Ivory mixed with oil and Rasanjan and applied on the area promotes hair growth there.

Also the Mashi of Nails, Bones, Skin, Horns, and Toes of four legged animals is useful for the purpose of **Romasanjanana.**

3. Krushnikarana

This has been indicated for curing the white patches resulting after wound healing or after any other disease.

'Bakuch' is considered to be the best for this purpose. External application of the seeds of these plant are beneficial.

4. Avasadan

This is useful for removing the hypergranulated tissue of the scar. This is beneficial for 'Keloids'.

Jasmine buds, Hirakas, Manasheel, Hartal, Guggul, Chitrak are used for Avasdan

उत्सन्नमांसान् व्रणानामवसादनम्।
जातीमुकुलकासीसमनोह्वालपुराग्निकैः॥

अष्टांगहृदय–उत्तरस्थान 25/48

The hypergranulated tissue which is hard, elevated chronic, has itching sensation and in which Shodhankarma cannot be done. In such cases Ksharakarma should be done.

उत्सन्नमांसान् कठिनान् कण्डूयुक्तांश्चिरोत्थितान्।
व्रणान्सुदुःखशोध्याश्च योर्जयत्क्षारकर्मणा॥

अष्टांगहृदय–उत्तरस्थान

5. Utsadan

For filling up the deep scars, dry, deep scar can be filled by using Nyagrodhadi, Padmakdi gana, Askand, Chikanamool, Sessame.

Eating flesh of carnivorous animals is also very useful.

शुष्कात्यमांसे गम्भीरे व्रणे उत्सादनं हितम्।
न्यग्रोधपद्मकादिभ्यामश्वगन्धाबलातिलैः॥
अद्यान्मांसादमांसानि विश्विनोपहितानि च।
मांसं मांसादमांसेन वर्धते शुद्धचेतसः॥

अष्टांगहृदय–उत्तरस्थान 25/46–47

CHAPTER 26

PRACTICAL APPLICATION OF BASIC PRINCIPALS OF AYURVEDA IN AYURVEDIC COSMETOLOGY

Dr. Manish Patwardhan

वृद्धिः समानैः सर्वेषां विपरीतैर्विपर्ययः।

अष्टांगहृदय–उत्तरस्थान 1/14

The Property of Dravya Samanyatwa (oneness) has been applied in the treatment of 'Romasanjanana'. There oneness (Dravyasamanytwa) of Hair and Mashi of Nails, Bones, Horns, toes of four legged animals is used for the Vrudhi (increase) *i.e.,* promote growth of Hair (वृद्धिः समानैः)

The Property of Dravya Samanyatwa (oneness) is applied in the 'Utsadan' indicated in deep scars. There to fill up the deep scars with the 'Mansadhatu'—They have told to eat meat (Mansa dhatu) of carnivorous animals. (वृद्धिः समानैः)

सर्वदा सर्वभावानां सामान्यं वृद्धिकारणम्।
ह्रासहेतुर्विशेषश्च, प्रवृत्तिरुभयस्य तु॥

चरक संहिता–सूत्रस्थान 1/46

Name of the Herb : Turmeric (हरिद्रा) Haridra

Rasa : Tikta (Bitter), Katu (Pungent)

Virya : Ushna (Hot)

Vipaka : Katu (Pungent)

Guna-Dharma (Properties)	:	Ruksha, Laghu, (Dry Light)
Route: Ext. Application Oral		
Uses(Concerning Skin Only)	:	Ext. Application-Kustha (dermatitis), Kandu (pruritus), Varna Prasadan (skinglow) would healing, coagulating blood. Oral : One of the best Treatment for Shitpitta (Allergy)

Name of the Herb	:	Indian Berberry (दारुहरिद्रा) Daruharidra
Rasa	:	Tikta (Astringent), Kashaya
Virya	:	Ushna (Hot)
Vipaka	:	Katu (Pungent)
Guna-Dharma (Properties)	:	Ruksha (Desicant), Laghu (Light)
Route	:	Oral
Uses (Concerning Skin only)	:	Internally—Blood purifier & hence cures skin diseases caused due to impurities of blood. VARNA PRASADAN. (Colour improver)

Name of the Herb	:	Bird Cherry (पद्मक) (Padmaka)
Rasa	:	Tikta (Bitter), Kashaya (Astringent)

Virya : Cold (Sheet)

Vipaka : Katu (Pungent)

Guna-Dharma (Properties) : Laghu (Light)

Route : External

Uses (Concerning Skin only) : Application improves complexion (Varnya), Kandughna (anti itching), Kusthaghna (cures dermatitis)

Name of the Herb : Nagkeshar (Mesua)

Rasa : Tikta (Bitter), Kashaya (Astringent)

Virya : Ushna (Hot)

Vipaka : Katu (Pungent)

Guna-Dharma (Properties) : Ruksha (Dry), Laghu (Light)

Route : External

Uses (Concerning Skin only) : Application helpfull in decreasing bad odour due to excessive sweating, Varna Prasadan (वर्ण्य) (Improves colour).

Name of the Herb : Keshar (Saffron)

Rasa : Katu (Pungent), Tikta (Bitter)

Virya : Ushna (Hot)

Vipaka : Katu (pungent)

Guna-Dharma (Properties)	:	Snigdha (Oily)
Route	:	External
Uses (Concerning Skin only)	:	Application is Varnya (Improves complexion)

Name of the Herb	:	Ushir (Khaskhas grass)
Rasa	:	Tikta (Bitter), Madhur (Sweet)
Virya	:	Sheet (Cold)
Vipaka	:	Katu (pungent)
Guna-Dharma (Properties)	:	Ruksha (Dry), Laghu (Light)
Route	:	External and Internal
Uses (Concerning Skin only)	:	Application has cooling, soothing effect on skin. It is varnya (good for colour), Helpfull in various skin diseases. Rakta Prasadan *i.e.*, purifies blood and cures various skin diseases due to blood impurities, KUSTHGHNA (dermatitis).

Name of the Herb	:	Rakta Chandan (Red sanders)
Rasa	:	Tikta (bitter), Madhur (Sweet)
Virya	:	Sheet (Cold)
Vipaka	:	Katu (pungent)
Guna-Dharma (Properties)	:	Ruksha (Dry), Guru (Heavy)

Route	:	External and Internal
Uses (Concerning Skin only)	:	External Application--Cooling effect on skin, cures various skin anamolies. Internal–Rakta Prasadan; KUSTHAGHNA

Name of the Herb	:	Chandan (Sandalwood)
Rasa	:	Tikta (Bitter), Madhur (Sweet)
Virya	:	Sheet (Cold)
Vipaka	:	Katu (Pungent)
Guna-Dharma (Properties)	:	Ruksha (Dry), laghu (Light)
Route	:	External and Internal
Uses (Concerning Skin only)	:	External Application–Removes body odour, varnya, cures various skin diseases, has cooling effect. Internal—KUSTHAGHNA, RAKTASHODHAK (Purifies blood)

Name of the Herb	:	Yashtimadhu (Liquorice)
Rasa	:	Madhur (Sweet)
Virya	:	Sheet (Cold)
Vipaka	:	Madhur (Sweet)
Guna-Dharma (Properties)	:	Guru (Heavy), Snigdha (Oily)

Route	:	External and Internal
Uses (Concerning Skin only)	:	Externally—gives soothing effect in burning sensation of skin. Internal—Varnya, cures various skin diseases, Kusthaghna.

Name of the Herb	:	Manjishtha (Indian madder)
Rasa	:	Tikta (bitter), Kashaya (Astringent), madhur (Sweet)
Virya	:	Ushna (Hot)
Vipaka	:	Katu (Pungent)
Guna-Dharma (Properties)	:	Guru (Heavy), Ruksha (Dry)
Route	:	External and Internal
Uses (Concerning Skin only)	:	External—Kusthaghna, Varnya Internal—Raktashodhak (purifies blood); cures Visarpa (Herpes) and other skin diseases.

Name of the Herb	:	Sariva (Anantmool)
Rasa	:	Madhur (Sweet)
Virya	:	Sheet (Cold)
Vipaka	:	Madhur (Sweet)
Guna-Dharma (Properties)	:	Guru (Heavy), Snigdha (Oily)
Route	:	External & Internal

Uses (Concerning Skin only)	:	Externally—Cooling effect on skin (Dahaprashamana)

Name of the Herb	:	Khadir (Cutch tree)
Rasa	:	Kashaya (Astringent), Tikta (Bitter)
Virya	:	Sheet (Cold)
Vipaka	:	Katu (Pungent)
Guna-Dharma (Properties)	:	Laghu (light), Ruksha (dry)
Route	:	External and Internal
Uses (Concerning Skin only)	:	External application–Kusthaghna, useful in treating eczema Internally also–Kusthaghna (Best)

Name of the Herb	:	Nimba (Neem) Margosa tree
Rasa	:	Tikta (Bitter), Kashaya (Astringent)
Virya	:	Sheet (Cold)
Vipaka	:	Katu (Pungent)
Guna-Dharma (Properties)	:	Laghu (Light)
Route	:	External and Internal
Uses (Concerning Skin only)	:	External—Disinfectant, wound healing (Vranropan), Kusthaghna Internal—Kusthaghna

Name of the Herb	:	Kustha Costus/Kuth
Rasa	:	Tikta, Katu (Pungent), Madhur (Sweet)
Virya	:	Ushna (Hot)
Vipaka	:	Katu (Pungent)
Guna-Dharma (Properties)	:	Laghu (Light), Ruksha (Dry), Tikshna
Route	:	External and Internal
Uses (Concerning Skin only)	:	External—Removes Body odour, Varnya, Kusthaghna. Internal—Purifies Blood (Rakta Shodak), Kusthaghna

---

Name of the Herb	:	Lodhra Symplocos racemosa
Rasa	:	Kashaya (Astringent)
Virya	:	Sheet (Cold)
Vipaka	:	Katu (Pungent)
Guna-Dharma (Properties)	:	Laghu (Light), Ruksha (Dry)
Route	:	External and Internal
Uses (Concerning Skin only)	:	External—Skin Diseases. Internal—Skin Diseases.

Name of the Herb	:	Jatiphala (Nutmeg)
Rasa	:	Tikta (Bitter), Katu (Pungent)

Virya	:	Ushna (Hot)
Vipaka	:	Katu (Pungent)
Guna-Dharma (Properties)	:	Laghu (Light), Tikshna
Route	:	External
Uses (Concerning Skin only)	:	External Application–Varna, Kusthaghna, Removes body odour (Durgandanashak)

Product Name	:	Gulkund (Pravalyukta)
Main Ingredients	:	Pravalpishti, Guduchi Satwa, Gulkand
Dose	:-	1 Spoon, 1-2 times with Milk/ Water
Uses	:	Burning sensation of skin, to minimise heat sensation in body, useful after Measles and Chicken-pox.

Product Name	:	Chyavanaprasha
Main Ingredients	:	Dashamula, Guduchi, Shatavari, Triphala, Vasa, Bala, Vidari Kand, Ashwagandha.
Dose	:	1 tea Spoon, 1-2 times with Milk/ Water.
Uses	:	Rasayana Kalpa; Decreases the aging process hence useful for Vali, Palit etc.

Product Name	:	Raktavardhak
Main Ingredients	:	Triphala, Trikatu, Shring Bhasma, Shouktic Bhasma, Suvarna Makshik Bhasma, Loha Bhasma, Shilajeet, Chyavanprasha.
Dose	:	1 Spoon, 2 times with Milk.
Uses	:	Rasayana Kalpa; hence useful for Vali Palit.

Product Name	:	Raktashodhak Vati
Main Ingredients	:	Shuddha Gandhak, Vanga Bhasma, Kajjali, Loha Bhasma, Abhrak Bhasma, Tamra Bhasma, Shilajeet, Guggulu.
Dose	:	2 Tabs 2-3 times with Milk
Uses	:	Blood born skin diseases, Kandu (Itching), Pruritis (Vicharchika) eczema etc.

Product Name	:	Sookshma Triphala
Main Ingredients	:	Triphala, Kajjali
Dose	:	1-2 Tabs, 2-3 times with Water
Uses	:	Rakta Shodhak (Blood purifier), Twacha Vikar (Dermatitis), Mukhadooshika (Acne) etc.

Product Name	:	Bhringraj Taila
Main Ingredients	:	Bhringaraj, Triphala, Sariva, Mandoor Privangu.
Dose	:	As required

Uses	:	Useful for body massage (Abhyanga).

Product Name	:	Padadari Malam
Main Ingredients	:	Tankanlahi, Kharpar, Sarjarus, Narikel Tail Vaseline Base.
Dose	:	Apply 2-3 times.
Uses	:	Cracks on Soles

Product Name	:	Lodhrasava
Main Ingredients	:	Lodhra, karchur, Kustha, Bhunimba, Vidang, Tagar, Nagkeshar, Triphala, Privangu etc.
Dose	:	2-4 spoons, 2 times with water after meals
Uses	:	Chronic skin diseases (Kushtha)

Product Name	:	Amrutarishta
Main Ingredients	:	Guduchi, Dashmool, Parpat, Musta, Trikatu, Nagkeshar
Dose	:	2-4 spoons after meals with Water
Uses	:	Raktadushti, Skin Diseases

Product Name	:	Vidangarishta
Main Ingredients	:	Vidang, Pippalimool, Rasna, Paripatha, Amalaki, Pippali, Twak Tail, Tamal Patra.
Dose	:	2-4 spoons after meals with Water.
Uses	:	Leucoderma

Product Name	:	Saraswatarishta
Main Ingredients	:	Brahmi, Shatavari, Vidari, Ashwagandha, Vidang, Guduchi, Kustha, Vacha, Usheer
Dose	:	2-3 spoons after meals with Water.
Uses	:	Brightens complexion (Varna Prasadan)

Product Name	:	Paripathadi Kadha
Main Ingredients	:	Paripatha, Indrayava, Bhunimba, Parpat, Guduchi, Shunthi, Musta
Dose	:	2-3 spoon after meals with Water.
Uses	:	Alergic rash, Reduces burning sensation of body/skin, Measles, Chickenpox

Product Name	:	Bhoonimbadi Quath
Main Ingredients	:	Bhunimb, Nimb, Triphala, Patol, Vasa, Guduchi
Dose	:	2-4 spoons after meals
Uses	:	Alergic rash, purifies blood

Product Name	:	Gandhak Rasayan (Barah Puti)
Main Ingredients	:	Gandhak, Godugdha, Twak, Tamalpatra, Ela, Nagkeshar, Guduchi, Triphala, Shunthi, Adrak, Bhringraj
Dose	:	1-2 Tabs, 2-3 times with Milk
Uses	:	All types of skin diseases

Product Name	: Laghusutashekhara
Main Ingredients	: Shunthi, Suvarnagairik, Nagwalli Patra Swaras
Dose	: 1-2 Tabs–2-3 times with Water
Uses	: Purpura, Itching, Allergic rash

Product Name	: Shankh Bhasma Vati
Main Ingredients	: Shankha Bhasma
Dose	: 2 Tabs, 2-3 times with warm Water
Uses	: Acne-pimples, Brightens complexion (Varṇya)

Product Name	: Triphala Choorna
Main Ingredients	: Haritaki, Bibhitak, Amalaki
Dose	: 1/2 to 1 spoon with warm Water, Honey, Ghee
Uses	: External application–Improves skin of colour

Product Name	: Chandan Bala Lakshadi Tail
Main Ingredients	: Chandan, Balamool, Laksha, Yashtimadhu, Ketaki, Ananta, Ela, Usheer, Devdaru, Kushtha Agaru, Musta, Champaka
Dose	: As required.
Uses	: Useful for daily body massage–Abhyanga

Product Name	:	Narayan Taila
Main Ingredients	:	Ashwagandha, Balamool, Bilwa-mool, Patala, Gokshur, Nimba, Punarnava, Chandan, Shatavari, Kostha
Dose	:	As required
Uses	:	Useful for daily body massage (Abhyanga)

Product Name	:	Vranaropak Taila.
Main Ingredients	:	Triphala, Haridra, Nimb, Bhuni-mb, Raktachandan
Dose	:	Apply 2-3 times.
Uses	:	Helps wound healing (fasten the process)

Product Name	:	Vranashodak Taila
Main Ingredients	:	Nirgudi, Karveer, Nimb, Dhattur, Haritaki
Dose	:	Apply 2-3 times
Uses	:	All types of infected wounds, Dandruff

Product Name	:	Bavachi Lep Goli
Main Ingredients	:	Bakuchi, Gomutra, (Bhavana)
Dose	:	External Application
Uses	:	Leucoderma, while patches due to any wound/disease

Product Name	:	Ushirasava
Main Ingredients	:	Usheer, Kamal, Gambhari, Priyangu, Lodhra, Manjishtha, Bhunimba, Karchur
Dose	:	2-4 Spoons after meals with water
Uses	:	Obstinate skin diseases, Burning sensation all over the body/skin

Product Name	:	Chandanasava
Main Ingredients	:	Chandan, Usheer, Musta, Padmaka, Lodhra, Manjishtha, Yashtimadhu, Raktachandan
Dose	:	2-4 Spoon after meals with Water
Uses	:	Raktavikar, Burning sensation

Product Name	:	Lohasava
Main Ingredients	:	Trikatu, Triphala, Ajmoda, Loha bhasma, Vidang
Dose	:	2-4 Spoons after meals
Uses	:	Chronic skin diseases, Kushtha

Product Name	:	Sarivadyasava
Main Ingredients	:	Sariva, Musta, Lodhra, Anantmool, Padmaka Patha
Dose	:	2-4 Spoons after meals
Uses	:	Skin diseases

Product Name	:	Khadirarishta
Main Ingredients	:	Khadir, Triphala, Bakuchi, Daruharidra, Nagkeshar

Dose	:	2-4 Spoons after meals
Uses	:	Obstinate skin diseases. Kushtha, Eczema, Dermatitis etc.

Product Name	:	Mahamanjishthadi Quath
Main Ingredients	:	Manjistha, Nimb, Triphala, Haridra, Khadir, Ananta
Dose	:	2-4 Spoons after meals
Uses	:	Rakta dushti, Skin Diseases, Itching, Leucoderma, Erysepalis etc.

Product Name	:	Amrutadi Guggul.
Main Ingredients	:	Guduchi, Patol, Triphala, Vidanga, Shunthi, Guggul.
Dose	:	2-3 Tabs, 2-3 times with warm Water.
Uses	:	Acne.

Product Name	:	Arogyavardhini
Main Ingredients	:	Kajjali, Lohabhasma, Tamra Bhasma, Shilajeet, Guggul, Abrak Bhasma, Chitrak, Katuka
Dose	:	1-3 Tabs, 2-3 times a day with warm Water
Uses	:	Skin diseases, various chronic and others due to Raktadushti

Product Name	:	Abhrak Bhasma
Main Ingredients	:	Krishna Abhraka

Dose	:	125-250 mg twice with honey, milk or ghee
Uses	:	Chronic skin diseases, improves complexion (Varnya)

Product Name	:	Loha Bhasma
Main Ingredients	:	Loha Bhasma
Dose	:	125-250 mg 2-3 times
Uses	:	Improves complexion (Varnya), obstinate skin diseases

Product Name	:	Suvarna Bhasma
Main Ingredients	:	Suvarna, Suvarna Makshik
Dose	:	60 mg. 2-3 times with honey
Uses	:	Chronic skin diseases, Varna Prasadan

Product Name	:	Utane Choorna
Main Ingredients	:	User, Kapurkachari, Kachora, Shweta Chandan, Nagarmotha
Dose	:	External Application as required
Uses	:	Varna Prasadan (Improves complexion), Removes bad body odour, Itching (Kandu) due to various skin diseases Dermatitis

DISEASE-WISE

Name of the Disease	:	Mukha-Dushika, Tarunya Pitika-Acne Pimples (Ref. 1A)

Pathology : Mostly in young people on face

Dosh-Dushti : Vata-Kapha

Symptoms : Pain

Treatment : Local Applications

1. Lodhra + Dhane + Vacha
2. Coconut Shell + Vata leaves
3. Vamankarma
4. Nasya
5. Blood letting from forehead (Ref No. 1B)

All the local applications given later also useful.

Ref No. 1(A)

शाल्मलीकण्टकाकारा: पिटिका: सरूजो घना:।
मेदोगर्भा मुखे यूनां ताभ्यां च मुखदूषिका:॥

अष्टांगहृदय उत्तरस्थान 31/5

1(B)

रोध्रकुस्तुम्बरूवचाप्रलेपो मुखदूषिके।
वटपल्लवयुक्ता वा नारीकेलोत्थशुक्तय:॥
अशान्तौ वमनं नस्यं ललाटे च शिराव्यध:

अष्टांगहृदय उत्तरस्थान 32/3

Name of the Disease : Til-Kalaka (Black Spots)

Pathology : Pitta Vikruti (Ideopathic)

Dosh-Dushti : Pitta-Vata

Symptoms : No Symptoms

Treatment	:	Burn in by Sun rays; Kshara; by Cautery (Ref. No. 2B)

Ref No. 2(A)

..................तिताथांस्तितकातकान्।
कृष्णानवेदनांस्त्वकस्थान...............॥

अष्टांगहृदय उत्तरस्थान 31/25

2(B)

दहेत्तु तिलकालकान्॥13॥
मषांश्च सूर्यकान्तेन क्षारेण यदि वाग्निना॥

अष्टांगहृदय उत्तरस्थान 32/13-15

Name of the Disease	:	Mashaka (Masa) (ref.3A)
Pathology	:	–
Dosh-Dushti	:	–
Symptoms	:	No Symptoms
Treatment	:	Same as above (Ref. 2B)

Ref. No. 3(A)

मषांस्तानेव चोन्नतान्।

Name of the Disease	:	(Ref. 4A)
Pathology	:	Krodha and Shoka etc. causes Vata-Pitta Vikruti and`they give rise to Blackish spots on the Face
Dosh-Dushti	:	Vata-Pitta
Symptoms	:	Itching, Burning sensation

Treatment :

1. Blood letting Ref. 4B
2. External Application Buds and Twaka of Kshiri Tress Ref. 4B.
3. External application Arjun/Manjishtha with Honey Ref. 4C.

Following External applications are also useful :

1. Rakta Chandan, Majishtha, Kustha, Lodhra, Ral, Masur, Vata Buds Ref. 4B.
2. Jeerak, Shahajeera, Sessame, Shiras in Milk Ref. 4E.
3. Leaves of mango and Jambu, Curd, Haridra, Jaggery Daruharidra Ref. No. 4F.

All the Treatment mentioned for above disease useful for mostly all skin diseases mentioned above.

Ref No. 4(A) :

शोकक्रोधादिकुपिताद्वात पित्तान्मुखे तनु।
श्यामलं मण्डलं व्यङगं.......................

अष्टांगहृदय उत्तरस्थान 31/28

Ref No. 4(B) :

...........कुर्याद्यथासन्नं शिराव्यधम्।
लेपयेत्क्षीरपिष्टैश्च क्षीरिवृक्षत्वमङ्कुरैः॥

अष्टांगहृदय उत्तरस्थान 32/15

Ref No. 4(C) :

व्यङ्गेषु चार्जुनत्वभ्वा मञ्जिष्ठा वा समाक्षिका।
लेपः सनवनीता वा श्वेताश्वखुरजा मषी॥

अष्टांगहृदय उत्तरस्थान 32/16

Ref No. 4(D) :

रक्तचन्दनमञ्जिष्ठाकुष्ठरोध्रप्रियङ्गवः।
वटाङ्कुरा मसूराश्च व्यङ्गघ्ना मुखकान्तिदाः॥

अष्टांगहृदय उत्तरस्थान 32/17

Ref No. 4(E) :

द्वे जीरके कृष्णातिलाः सर्षपाः पयसा सह।
पिष्टाः कुर्वन्ति वक्त्रेन्दुमपास्तव्यङ्गलाञ्छनम्॥

अष्टांगहृदय उत्तरस्थान 32/18

Ref No. 5(F) :

जम्ब्वाम्रपल्लवा मस्तुहरिद्रे द्वे नवो गुडः।
लेपः सवर्णकृत्पिष्टं स्वरसेन च तिन्दुकम॥

अष्टांगहृदय उत्तरस्थान 32/22

CHAPTER 27

AYURVEDA FRAGRANT HERBS

Dr. Mahesh Sabade

1. Karpoor	2. Kasturi
3. Latakasturi	4. Chandan
5. Agaru	6. Tagar
7. Padmakh	8. Jatiphal
9. Javitri	10. Lavang
11. Aela	12. Twak
13. Tamal patra	14. Nagkeshar
15. Kumkum	16. Ushir
17. Jatamansi	18. Musta
19. Karchoor	20. Talispatra
21. Karpoor	22. Kamal
23. Taruni	24. Bela
25. Chameli	26. Champak
27. Ketaki	

KARPOOR

Sanskrit Name : Karpoor

English Name : Camphor

Botanical Name : Borneo Camphor

Description : Bhimseni Karpoor is the best variety of camphor.

Characteristics

Rasa (Taste)	–	Bitter
Veerya (Potency)	–	Cool
Vipak (Postdigestive Effect)	–	Pungent
Guna (Properties)	–	Fragrant, light.

Doshaghnata : (Action on doshas) Alleviates Vata and Pitta.

Action and Indications

(*i*) It removes bad odour of mouth, sweat, urine and stool.

(*ii*) It has scraping action on dosha, dhatu and mala.

(*iii*) It acts as a cardiac stimulant.

(*iv*) It is beneficial in excessive thirst, vitiation of pitta.

(*v*) It is also beneficial in cough, breathlessness, diabetes, irritable bowel syndrome.

Preparations : (*a*) Karpooradi vati, (*b*) Karpooradi Choorna, (*c*) Karpoorasav, (*d*) Karpoor Rasa, (*e*) Krumikutharrasa, (*f*) Fortexforte.

Chemical Composition

It has stearoptenes – a kind of volatile oil.

KASTURÍ

Sanskrit Name : Kasturi

English Name : Musk

Botanical Name : Moschus Moschiferus

Description : It is collected from a specific variety of deer.

Characteristics

Rasa (Taste)	– Pungent, Bitter
Veerya (Potency)	– Hot
Vepak (Postdigestive effect)	– Pungent
Guna (Properties)	– Heavy, Fragrant

Doshaghnata : (Action on Doshas) In alleviates vata and Kapha

Action and Indications

(*i*) It acts as an antidote of toxins.

(*ii*) It gives strength to heart and brain.

(*iii*) It acts as an aphrodisiac.

(*iv*) Reduces foul smell and oedema.

(*v*) It is beneficial in convulsions, Kapha and Vata disorders.

Preparations: (*a*) Kasturi Bhairav Rasa, (*b*) Mrugamadasava.

Chemical Composition : It has must xylene, musk ketone etc.

LATAKASTURI

Sanskrit Name : Latakasturi

English Name : Musk Mallow

Botanical Name : Hibiscus Abelmoschus

Description : The seeds of this plant have fragrance similar to Kasturi.

Characteristics

Rasa (Taste)	– Bitter
Veerya (Potency)	– Cool
Vipak (Postdigestive effect)	– Sweet
Guna (Properties)	– Light, Fragrant

Doshaghnata : (Action on Doshas) Alleviates Kapha and Pitta.

Action and Indications

(*i*) It increases agni.

(*ii*) Gives strength.

(*iii*) Relieves thirst.

(*iv*) It is beneficial in disorders of kapha, eyes and urinary bladder.

(*v*) It acts as an aphrodisiac.

(*vi*) It also acts as an cardiac stimulant and gives strength.

(*vii*) Local application relieves itch. It is used to make other oils fragrant.

Preparations : Udwartan

Chemical Composition : It has volatile oil, gum resin, albumin.

CHANDAN

Sanskrit Name : Chandan

English Name : Sandal Wood

Botanical Name : Santalum Album

Description : The inner wood or heart wood is kept to mature. This improves the fragrance of the sandal wood. The oil is extracted from the wood by distillation method.

Characteristics

Rasa (Taste)	–	Bitter
Veerya (Potency)	–	Cool
Vipak (Postdigestive effect)	–	Pungent
Guna (Properties)	–	Dry, Fragrant.

Doshaghnata : (Action on Doshas) Alleviates Pitta and Kapha.

Action and Indications

(*i*) It relieves burning sensation, excessive thirst and itching.

(*ii*) It acts as a diuretic.

(*iii*) The oil from it stimulates kidneys, generates urine.

(*iv*) Sandal wood relieves offensive body odour.

(*v*) Acts as an aphrodisiac.

(*vi*) It is beneficial in urinary tract infection, burning micturation, skin disorders, diabetes.

Preparations : (*a*) Chandanasav, (*b*) Chandanadivati, (*c*) Chandanbalakshadi Oil.

Chemical Composition : The bark has volatile oil, tanic acid, and gum resin.

AGARU

Sanskrit Name : Agaru, Aguru

English Name : Eagle Wood

Botanical Name : Aquilaria Agallocha

Description : The fragrance is present in the stem *i.e.,* The wooden part of the tree.

Characteristics

Rasa (Taste)	–	Pungent, Bitter
Veerya (Potency)	–	Hot
Vepak (Postdigestive effect)	–	Pungent
Guna (Properties)	–	Sharp, Light, Fragrance.

Doshaghnata : (Action on Doshas) Alleviates Vata and Kapha.

Action and Indications

(*i*) It stimulates the nervous system.

(*ii*) Acts as an aphrodisiac.

(*iii*) A geriatric medicine.

(*iv*) It is beneficial in breathlessness.

(*v*) Skin disorders.

(*vi*) Gout Rheumatoid Arthritis.

(*vii*) Hiccup.

Preparations : Udvartan (Utane), Chyawanprash.

Chemical Composition : It has a volatile oil which dissolves in ether.

TAGAR

Sanskrit Name : Tagar

English Name : Indian Valerian Rhizome

Botanical Name : Valeriana Wallichii

Description : The fragrance is present in the roots of the herb.

Characteristics

Rasa (Taste)	– Sweet
Veerya (Potency)	– Hot
Vepak (Postdigestive effect)	– Sweet
Guna (Properties)	– Unctuous, Light Fragrant.

Doshaghnata : (Action on Doshas) Alleviates all the three dosha.

Action and Indications

(*i*) It is beneficial in convulsions, Opthalamic disorders and Poisoning.

(*ii*) It acts as an analgesic.

(*iii*) Helps in insomnia and Psychological disorders.

(*iv*) It is also beneficial in rheumatoid arthritis, osteo arthiritis, Gout etc.

Preparations : Prasham

Chemical Composition : It has volatile oil, containing sesquiterpenes, valeric acid, terpene alcohol.

PADMAKH

Sanskrit Name : Padmakh, Padmak

English Name : Mild Himalaya Cherry

Botanical Name : Prunus Puddum

Description : Dried stem has a very good fragrance. Though it is light by weight it is hard to make powder.

Characteristics

Rasa (Taste)	– Astringent, Bitter

Veerya (Potency) – Cool

Vepak (Postdigestive effect) – Katu (Pungent)

Guna (Properties) – Light, Fragrance.

Doshaghnata : (Action on Doshas) Alleviates Pitta and Kapha. It increases Vata.

Action and Indications

(*i*) It acts as an analgesic.

(*ii*) An antidote to toxins.

(*iii*) It is beneficial in the growth of the foetus.

(*iv*) It gives strength to the body, especially to rasa and asthi dhatu.

(*v*) It has an inhibitory action on vomiting and bleeding.

Preparations : Chandan–bala lakshadi oil.

Chemical Composition : It has hydrocyanic acid in its bark and also amygdalin.

JATIPHAL

Sanskrit Name : Jatiphal

English Name : Nutmeg

Botanical Name : Myristica Fragrance

Description : This is a commonly used spice. It is found in the fruit of the herb.

Characteristics

Rasa (Taste) – Bitter

Veerya (Potency) – Hot

Vepak (Postdigestive effect) – Pungent

Guna (Properties) – Sharp, Light, Fragrance

Doshaghnata : (Action on Doshas) Alleviates Kapha and Vata.

Action and Indications

(*i*) It improves the appetite.

(*ii*) Relieves foul smell of stools.

(*iii*) Relieves bad breath and Body odour.

(*iv*) It is beneficial in worm infestation.

(*v*) Cough.

(*vi*) Vomiting.

(*vii*) Breathlessness.

(*viii*) Weakness.

(*ix*) Rhinitis.

(*x*) Diarrhoea.

(*xi*) Cardiac disorders.

(*xii*) Being fragrant it acts as an aphrodisiac.

(*xiii*) It is also used for the treatment of premature ejaculation.

(*xiv*) Insomnia.

Preparations : Shankhodar, Khadiradi Vati, Urja.

Chemical Composition : It has light yellow coloured volatile–oil and a thick oily substance called nutmeg butter. Volatile oil contains eugenol and iso–eugenol.

JAVITRI

Sanskrit Name : Javitri, Jatipatri.

English Name : Mace

Botanical Name : Myristica fragrance.

Description : Javitri is outer covering of nutmeg. It is brownish red in colour.

Characteristics

Rasa (Taste)	–	Sweet, Pungent
Veerya (Potency)	–	Hot
Vepak (Postdigestive effect)	–	Pungent
Guna (Properties)	–	Light, Fragrant.

Doshaghnata : (Action on Doshas) Alleviates Kapha and Vata.

Action and Indications

(*i*) It acts as an appetiser.

(*ii*) Digestive.

(*iii*) It improves complexion.

(*iv*) Cough.

(*v*) Breathlessness.

(*vi*) Irritable bowel syndrome.

(*vii*) Worm infestation.

(*viii*) It also acts as an aphrodisiac medicine.

Preparations : Khadiradi Guti

Chemical Composition : It has a volatile oil alongwith sugar, dextrine, etc.

LAVANG

Sanskrit Name : Lavang, Devakusum

English Name : Clove

Botanical Name : Caryophyllus Aromaticus

Description : Clove is the dried bud of this plant.

Characteristics

Rasa (Taste)	– Pungent, Bitter
Veerya (Potency)	– Cool
Vepak (Postdigestive effect)	– Katu (Pungent)
Guna (Properties)	– Light, Fragrant

Doshaghnata : (Action on Doshas) Alleviates Kapha and Pitta.

Action and Indications

(*i*) It improves the appetite and digestion.

(*ii*) Gives taste.

(*iii*) It is beneficial in disorders of the blood.

(*iv*) Excessive thirst.

(*v*) Vomiting.

(*vii*) Flatulance.

(*vii*) Cough.

(*viii*) Breathlessness.

(*ix*) Hiccup.

Preparations : Lavangadi Vati, Aeladi Choornam, Avipatti-karchurna.

Chemical Composition : It has 15 – 20% volatile oil which contains 85 – 92% eugenol, galotanic acid and caryophyllene.

ELA

Sanskrit Name : Ela

English Name : Cardamom

Botanical Name : Elettaria Cardamomum

Description : There are two varieties of cardamom — (*i*) Greater, (*ii*) Lesser. The fruit and the seeds have a pleasant smell.

Characteristics

Rasa (Taste)	–	Pungent
Veerya (Potency)	–	Cool
Vepak (Postdigestive effect)	–	Pungent
Guna (Properties)	–	Light, Fragrant.

Doshaghnata : (Action on Doshas) Alleviates Kapha and Vata.

Action and Indications

(*i*) It acts as appetiser.

(*ii*) Digestive.

(*iii*) Being fragrant it stimulates the sense organs.

(*iv*) It has a specific action of urinary system and hence used in disorders of urinary system.

(*v*) Cough.

(*vi*) Breathlessness.

(*vii*) Haemorrhoids.

(*viii*) Urinary Calculus and Infections.

Preparations : Eladi Choorna, Eladi Vati.

Chemical Composition : It has 3 – 8% volatile oil which contains terpinene, terpineol, terpinyl acetate and cineol in less quantity.

TWAK

Sanskrit Name : Twak, Darusita

English Name : Cinnamon Bark

Botanical Name : Cinnamomum zeylanicum

Description : The bark of the tree is fragrant and used as medicine.

Characteristics

Rasa (Taste)	– Pungent
Veerya (Potency)	– Cool
Vipak (Postdigestive effect)	– Pungent.
Guna (Properties)	– Light, Fragrant.

Doshaghnata : (Action on Doshas) Allcviates Kapha and Pitta.

Action and Indications

(*i*) It acts as appetiser.

(*ii*) Digestive.

(*iii*) It stimulates and gives strength to the uterus.

(*iv*) It is used in amenorrhoea.

(*v*) Dysmenorrhoea.

(*vi*) It acts as an aphrodisiac.

(*vii*) It is beneficial in excessive thirst.

(*viii*) Dryness of mouth.

(*ix*) It increases WBC count in the blood.

(*x*) It cleanses the wounds.

(*xi*) Relieves pain.

Preparations : Sitopladi Choorna.

Chemical Composition : It has 0.5 – 1% of volatile oil, tannin and gum. The oil has cinnamaldehyde, eugenol, and following in less quantities methyl–amyl ketone, p–cymene, 1–Philandrene, L–a–pinene, L–linalool, cumic aldelyde, nonyl aldeluyde, caryophylline and esters of butyric acid.

TAMAL–PATRA

Sanskrit Name : Tamal Patra, Patra

English Name : Tamala

Botanical Name : Cinnamomum Tamala

Description : It is found in Indian and Srilanka.

Characteristics

Rasa (Taste)	–	Sweet.
Veerya (Potency)	–	Hot
Vepak (Postdigestive effect)	–	Pungent
Guna (Properties)	–	Sharp, Light, Fragrant.

Doshaghnata : (Action on Doshas) Alleviates Kapha and Vata.

Action and Indications

(*i*) It is beneficial in haemorrhoids.

(*ii*) Tastelessness.

(*iii*) Rhinitis.

(*iv*) It is used in indigestion.

(*v*) Abdominal pain.

(*vi*) Flatulance.

(*vii*) It tones the uterus which prevents abortion.

(*viii*) It generates sweat and urine.

Preparations : Chyawanprash.

Chemical Composition : It has a volatile oil with fragrance similar to clove oil.

NAG KESHAR

Sanskrit Name : Nagpushpa, Nagkeshar

English Name : Cobra's Saffron

Botanical Name : Mesua Ferrea

Description : This is found in Himalayas, Southern part of India, Bangaladesh etc.

Characteristics

Rasa (Taste)	–	Astringent
Veerya (Potency)	–	Hot
Vepak (Postdigestive effect)	–	Pungent
Guna (Properties)	–	Dry, Light.

Doshaghnata : (Action on Doshas) Alleviates kapha and Pitta.

Action and Indications

(*i*) Being hot potent it digest 'aam'

(*ii*) It relieves excessive thirst.

(*iii*) Itching.

(*iv*) Excessive sweating.

(*v*) Nausea.

(*vi*) Foul smell.

(*vii*) It is also beneficial in skin disorders.

(*viii*) Herpes.

(*ix*) Bleeding.

(*x*) Haemorrhoids.

(*xi*) Rhinitis.

(*xii*) Oil prepared from the seeds has analgesic action on local application.

Preparations : Vrushya Vati, Pushyanug Choorna.

Chemical Composition : Fruits have fragrant, Yellow coloured oil.

KUMKUM – SAFFRON

Sanskrit Name : Kumkum

English Name : Saffron

Botanical Name : Crocus sativus

Description : Saffron cultivated in Kashmir and Spain is one of the best varieties found. It has a very good fragrance.

Characteristics

Rasa (Taste)	–	Pungent, Bitter
Veerya (Potency)	–	Hot
Vepak (Postdigestive effect)	–	Pungent
Guna (Properties)	–	Unctuous

Doshaghnata : (Action on Doshas) Alleviates all the three doshas.

Action and Indications

(*i*) It acts as digestive.

(*ii*) Appetiser.

(*iii*) It improves the complexion.

(*iv*) Gives strength.

(*v*) Acts as an aphrodisiac.

(*vi*) Diuretic.

(*vii*) Mild Analgesic.

(*viii*) It is beneficial in urinary disorders.

(*ix*) Diarrhoea.

(*x*) Amenorrhoea.

(*xi*) Dysmenorrhoea.

(*xii*) Cough.

(*xiii*) Breathlessness.

(*xiv*) Shiroraga (various types of headache) etc.

Preparations : Kumkumadi Tailam.

Chemical Composition : It has stationary oil, volatile oil, picrocrocin, crocetin, crocin.

USHIR

Sanskrit Name : Ushir

English Name : Cuscus grass

Botanical Name : Andropogon muricatu Vetiveria Zizanioides.

Description : Ushir is the root of a kind of grass called veeran. It makes water fragrant.

Characteristics

Rasa (Taste)	–	Bitter, Sweet.
Veerya (Potency)	–	Cool
Vepak (Postdigestive effect)	–	Pungent.
Guna (Properties)	–	Light, Fragrant.

Doshaghnata : (Action on Doshas) Alleviates Kapha and Pitta.

Action and Indications

(*i*) It is cool potent.

(*ii*) Digestive in nature.

(*iii*) It is beneficial in fever.

(*iv*) Vomiting.

(*v*) Excessive thirst.

(*vi*) Poisoning.

(*vii*) Herps.

(*viii*) Urinary Infections.

(*ix*) Wounds.

(*x*) It acts as a galactogogue.

(*xi*) Being fragrant, it relieves the bad odour of the sweat.

Preparations : Ushirasav

Chemical Composition : It has volatile fragrant oil, gumresin, acids, etc.

JATAMANSI

Sanskrit Name : Jatamansi

English Name : Spike nard, Indian nard.

Botanical Name : Nardostachys Jatamansi.

Description : The roots of this plant are used as medicine. This is found in Himalayas, Sikkim and Bhutan.

Characteristics

Rasa (Taste)	–	Bitter, Astringent
Veerya (Potency)	–	Cool
Vepak (Postdigestive effect)	–	Sweet
Guna (Properties)	–	Fragrant

Doshaghnata : (Action on Doshas) Alleviates all the three doshas.

Action and Indications

(*i*) It acts as digestive.

(*ii*) Appetiser.

(*iii*) Diuretic.

(*iv*) Mild Laxative.

(*v*) Analgesic.

(*vi*) Blood Purifier.

(*vii*) It improves the blood circulation.

(*viii*) Gives strength to the heart.

(*ix*) Helps in relieving insomnia.

(*x*) It is beneficial in amenorrhoea.

(*xi*) Dysmenorrhoea.

(*xii*) Herpes.

(*xiii*) Skin disorders.

(*xiv*) It increases the grasping capacity.

(*xv*) Improves memory.

Preparations : Prasham shanti.

Chemical Composition : It has 0.3 – 0.4% volatile oil. Alongwith this oil it has ester, alcohol, seski terpene.

MUSTA

Sanskrit Name : Mustak

English Name : Nutgrass

Botanical Name : Cyperus Rotundus

Description : Musta is commonly found near water bodies.

Characteristics

Rasa (Taste)	–	Pungent, Bitter, Astringent.
Veerya (Potency)	–	Cool
Vepak (Postdigestive effect)	–	Pungent
Guna (Properties)	–	Fragrant

Doshaghnata : (Action on Doshas) Alleviates Kapha and Pitta.

Action and Indications

(*i*) It is appetiser.

(*ii*) Digestive.

(*iii*) Helps in diarrhoea.

(*iv*) It is beneficial is disorders of blood.

(*v*) Fever.

(*vi*) Tastiness.

(*vii*) Worm, infestation.

(*viii*) Excessive thirst.

(*ix*) It generates sweat.

(*x*) Urine.

(*xi*) Menses.

(*xii*) Stimulates uterus.

(*xiii*) It also acts as galactogogue.

(*xiv*) It is good for hair.

Preparations : Navayas Loha

Chemical Composition : It has a volatile oil, fat, sugar, gum resin, carbohydrates.

KARCHOOR

Sanskrit Name : Karchoor

English Name : Zedoary

Botanical Name : Curcuma Zedoari

Description : This is commonly found in Himalayas and Myanmar.

Characteristics

Rasa (Taste)	– Pungent, Bitter.
Veerya (Potency)	– Hot.
Vepak (Postdigestive effect)	– Pungent
Guna (Properties)	– Light, Fragrant.

Doshaghnata : (Action on Doshas) Alleviates Kapha and Vata.

Action and Indications

(*i*) It is appetiser.

(*ii*) Relieves tastelessness.

(*iii*) It is beneficial in skin disorders.

(*iv*) Haemorrhoids.

(*v*) Cough.

(*vi*) Breathlessness.

(*vii*) Worm infestation.

Preparations : Udvartan (Utane)

Chemical Composition : It has a volatile oil, pungent soft gum resin, starch, sugar and organic acid.

TALISPATRA

Sanskrit Name : Talis Patra

English Name : Himalayan Yew

Botanical Name : Taxus Baccata

Description : This is used as a spice in cooking. Found in Punjab, Kaṣhmir and Afganistan.

Characteristics

Rasa (Taste)	– Pungent
Veerya (Potency)	– Hot
Vepak (Postdigestive effect)	– Pungent.
Guna (Properties)	– Light, Fragrant.

Doshaghnata : (Action on Doshas) Alleviates Vata and Kapha.

Action and Indications

(*i*) It is beneficial in breathlessness.

(*ii*) Cough.

(*iii*) Tastelessness.

(*iv*) Amenorrhoea.

(*v*) Dysmenorrhoea.

(*vi*) It acts as an appetiser.

(*vii*) Digestive.

Preparations : Talisadi Choorna.

Chemical Composition : It has taxons present in the leaves.

SHEETALCHINI

Sanskrit Name : Kankol, Sheetalchini.

English Name : Cubebs, Tailed Pepper.

Botanical Name : Pipper Cubeba.

Description : This is the dried fruit of a creeper.

Characteristics

Rasa (Taste)	–	Bitter
Veerya (Potency)	–	Hot
Vepak (Postdigestive effect)	–	Pungent
Guna (Properties)	–	Light, Fragrant.

Doshaghnata : (Action on Doshas) Alleviates Vata and Kapha.

Action and Indications

(*i*) It gives taste.

(*ii*) Relatives bad breath.

(*iii*) It gives cooling effect on chewing.

(*iv*) It is beneficial in cardiac disorders.

(*v*) Stammering.

(*vi*) Excessive thirst.

(*vii*) Urinary disorders.

Preparations : Tambul.

Chemical Composition : It has volatile oil cubebin, starch, gum resin, cubebic acid, calcium oxalate, phosphate.

KAMAL SACRED LOTUS

Sanskrit Name : Kamal, Padma,

English Name : Sacred Lotus.

Botanical Name : Nelumbium speciousum

Description : This is an aquatic plant. The roots of this plant grow in the mud.

Characteristics

Rasa (Taste)	–	Sweet
Veerya (Potency)	–	Cool
Vepak (Postdigestive effect)	–	Sweet
Guna (Properties)	–	Fragrant.

Doshaghnata : (Action on Doshas) Alleviates Kapha and Pitta.

Action and Indications

(*i*) It is beneficial in burning sensation.

(*ii*) Skin disorders.

(*iii*) Herpes.

(*iv*) Poisoning.

(*v*) Cardiac disorders.

(*vi*) Urinary disorders.

Preparations : Arvindasav

Chemical Composition : It has gum resin, glucose, metarbin, tannin, nelumbine.

ROSE – TARUNI

Sanskrit Name : Taruni

English Name : Rose

Botanical Name : Rosa centifolia

Description : Various varieties of rose are found almost every where.

Characteristics

Rasa (Taste)	– Bitter
Veerya (Potency)	– Cool
Vepak (Postdigestive effect)	– Pungent
Guna (Properties)	– Fragrant, Light.

Doshaghnata : (Action on Doshas) Alleviates all the three doshas.

Action and Indications

(*i*) It is digestive.

(*ii*) Mild laxative.

(*iii*) It improves complexion.

(*iv*) It is beneficial in skin.

(*v*) Cardiac disorders.

Preparations : Gulkand, Gulab Arka.

Chemical Composition : It has volatile oil, tanic acid, malic acid, and gum resin.

BELA

Sanskrit Name : Bela, Varshiki

English Name : Jasmine

Botanical Name : Jasminum Sambac

Description : These are the fragrant followers with four varieties.

Characteristics

Rasa (Taste)	–	Bitter
Veerya (Potency)	–	Cool
Vepak (Postdigestive effect)	–	Pungent
Guna (Properties)	–	Light.

Doshaghnata : (Action on Doshas) Alleviates all the three doshas.

Action and Indications

(*i*) It relieves oedema on feet and on the breast.

(*ii*) The paste of flowers is applied on the breast in oedema due to stagnation of breast milk.

(*iii*) It stimulates the uterus.

Chemical Composition : It has volatile oil present in it.

CHAMELI

Sanskrit Name : Malati, Svarnajati

English Name : Spanish Jasmine

Botanical Name : Jasminum grandiflorum

Description : These are fragrant flowers.

Characteristics

Rasa (Taste)	– Bitter, Astringent
Veerya (Potency)	– Hot
Vepak (Postdigestive effect)	– Pungent
Guna (Properties)	– Light.

Doshaghnata : (Action on Doshas) Alleviates Vata and Kapha Doshas.

Action and Indications

(*i*) It is beneficial in the disorders of head.

(*ii*) Eyes.

(*iii*) Mouth.

(*iv*) Skin disorders.

Preparations :

Chemical Composition : It has salicylic acid.

CHAMPAK

Sanskrit Name : Champak, Champa

English Name : Champak

Botanical Name : Michelia Champaca

Description : This is a yellow coloured fragrant flower.

Characteristics

Rasa (Taste)	– Pungent, Bitter, Astringent, Sweet.

Veerya (Potency) – Cool

Vepak (Postdigestive effect) – Pungent

Guna (Properties) – Fragrant.

Doshaghnata : (Action on Doshas) Alleviates all the three doshas.

Action and Indications

(*i*) It is beneficial in skin.

(*ii*) Opthalmic disorders.

(*iii*) Gout.

Preparations :

Chemical Composition : Volatile oil is present in the flowers.

KETAKI

Sanskrit Name : Ketaki, Suvarnaketaki.

English Name : Screw Pine.

Botanical Name : Pandanus Odoratissimus.

Description : This frangrant flower is easily found in the coastal parts of India.

Characteristics

Rasa (Taste) – Pungent, Sweet.

Veerya (Potency) – Hot

Vepak (Postdigestive effect) – Pungent

Guna (Properties) – Light, Fragrant.

Doshaghnata : (Action of Doshas) Alleviates Kapha.

Action and Indications

(*i*) It is beneficial in opthalmic disorders.

(*ii*) It gives strength to brain.

(*iii*) Relieves bad odour.

Preparations :

Chemical Composition : It has volatile oil present in the flower.